To Betty,

Happy Flowermaking!

Best Wishes

June '98

FLORAL
WEDDING
CAKES
& SPRAYS

Floral Wedding Cakes & Sprays

Alan Dunn

CONTENTS

Entries in *italics* indicate actual flower instructions

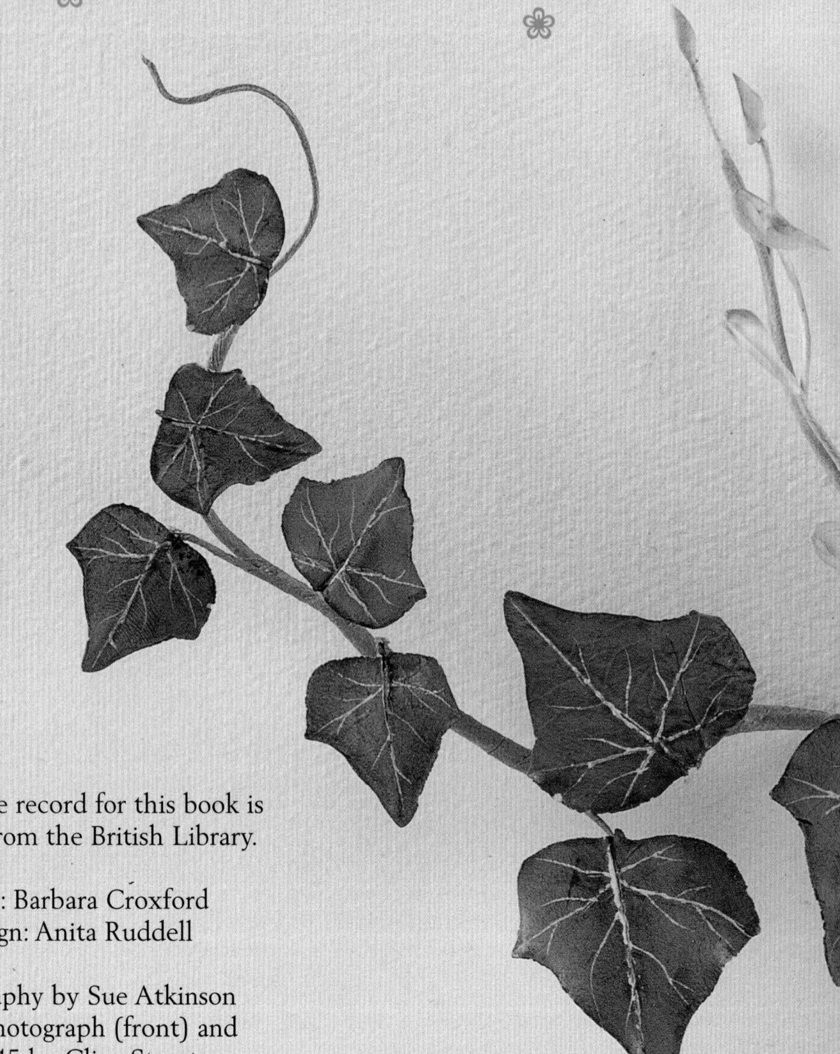

First published by
Merehurst Limited, 1998
Ferry House, 51–57 Lacy Road,
Putney, London SW15 1PR

ISBN 1-85391-604-8

A catalogue record for this book is available from the British Library.

Editor: Barbara Croxford
Design: Anita Ruddell

Photography by Sue Atkinson
Jacket photograph (front) and page 145 by Clive Streeter

Publisher: Anne Wilson

Colour separation by Bright Arts, Hong Kong

Printed and bound by Jarrold Book Printing, Thetford, Norfolk, England

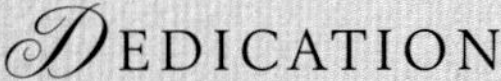

Dedication

With love to my Grandad, Ernest Blair, and to the memory of Mitz, the special dog with the very alternative sense of humour!

INTRODUCTION

Wedding cakes date back to Roman times when a basic fruit cake, made from food that was offered to the gods – rich fruit, nuts and honey cake – was used as part of the wedding ceremony. The cake was crumbled over the bride's head so that the gods would bless her with an abundance of everything. When Julius Caesar conquered Great Britain in 54 BC, the wedding cake, along with many other Roman traditions, was introduced and became part of our custom. It was only wealthy families at first who copied this practice, with poorer families scattering grains of wheat or corn over the bride, in the hope that their marriages too would be fertile. This custom carried on until about two hundred years ago.

The wedding cake has seen many changes since then, progressing very gradually to decorated cakes and then to multi-tiered centrepieces that many people now take for granted. To begin with, it was only royalty and the high society who could afford to have these tiered cakes, with the rest of the country having only single cakes decorated with perhaps a vase to add height to the display. The three-tier round cake became traditional, representing the three rings – the engagement, wedding and eternity ring. Soon the request for a three-tiered cake became fashionable amongst the middle classes, even if there was more cake than was actually needed for the guests. Consequently there was often a tier left over and, rather than use it immediately, it was often kept for the christening of the couple's first child.

Flowers too have been incorporated into celebrations and religious ceremonies since early times. So it therefore seems to have been a natural progression that flowers should feature quite predominantly in wedding cake designs. The styles of wedding cakes have evolved constantly over the years, with the fashions and trends of each period reflecting the cake design. In the past they were created as very grand formal tiered cakes, often inspired by architecture. Present day designs are more informal and less rigid in their design, and are often displayed on various types of cake stands. Flowers now, more than ever before, are often the main focal point of a wedding cake. The variation of sugar flowers and foliage used on cakes is vast, mainly due to the increased selection of flowers available to the florist which in turn can be offered to the bride.

In this book I have included a varied collection of some of the more unusual flowers, as well as many traditional flowers and foliage. The cake designs and floral combinations pictured in the

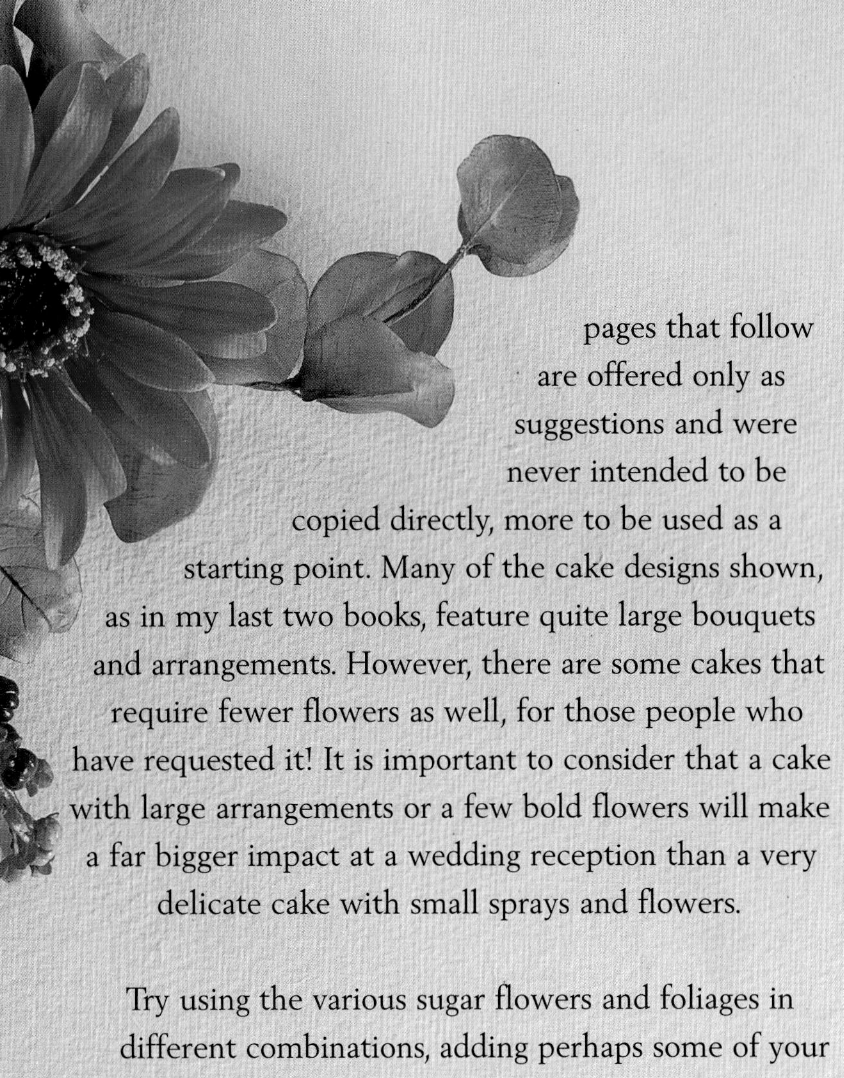

pages that follow are offered only as suggestions and were never intended to be copied directly, more to be used as a starting point. Many of the cake designs shown, as in my last two books, feature quite large bouquets and arrangements. However, there are some cakes that require fewer flowers as well, for those people who have requested it! It is important to consider that a cake with large arrangements or a few bold flowers will make a far bigger impact at a wedding reception than a very delicate cake with small sprays and flowers.

Try using the various sugar flowers and foliages in different combinations, adding perhaps some of your personal favourites. Use them to create and experiment to produce work that is as individual as you are. Remember that beauty is in the eye of the beholder and the only limit to what you can achieve is your own imagination; so get started and have fun!

Alan

HEAVENLY SCENT

A very simple, pretty cake design intended for a small wedding reception. The arrangement includes a charming combination of tuberoses, roses, rue leaves and ivy.

MATERIALS

25cm (10 in) oval cake
Apricot glaze
1.25kg (2½lb) almond paste (marzipan)
Clear alcohol (kirsch or vodka)
2kg (4lb) pale creamy-lemon sugarpaste
Royal icing coloured with primrose paste food colouring
Plum, white and holly/ivy petal dust (blossom tint)
Fine willow green ribbon to trim cake
Broad green velvet ribbon to trim board

EQUIPMENT

Sugarpaste smoothers
36cm (14 in) oval cake board
Nos. 1 and 42 piping tubes (tips)
Embroidery side design template (see page 154)

FLOWERS

Heavenly Scent Arrangement (see page 11)

CORSAGE

1 half rose and 1 rosebud (see page 136)
5 ivy leaves (see page 114)
1 piece of rue (see page 11)

PREPARATION

1 Brush the cake with apricot glaze and cover with almond paste. Leave to dry overnight. Moisten the almond paste with clear alcohol and then cover with creamy-lemon sugarpaste, using sugarpaste smoothers to create a good finish to the surface of the cake.

2 Cover the cake board with creamy-lemon sugarpaste and position the cake on top. Use the sugarpaste smoothers again to achieve a neat join between the base of the cake and the board. Allow to dry overnight.

3 Colour the royal icing with a small amount of primrose colouring to match the sugarpaste coating. Pipe a shell border around the base of the cake using the royal icing in a piping bag fitted with a no. 42 tube. Attach a band of fine willow green ribbon just above the shell border. Glue the broad velvet ribbon to the cake board edge using a non-toxic glue stick.

SIDE DESIGN

4 Either pipe the embroidery directly on to the cake using the pattern on page 154 as a guideline, or trace the design on to greaseproof (wax) paper and scribe it on to the cake first. Use a no.1 tube to pipe the design. Broderie anglaise 'holes' are made using the pointed end of a celstick and then an outline piped in royal icing. Allow the design to dry. Highlight the roses with a very pale mixture of plum and white petal dust. Highlight the leaves with holly/ivy petal dust.

ASSEMBLY

5 Make the Heavenly Scent arrangement as instructed on page 11, and position carefully on top of the cake. Wire a small corsage with the remaining roses, ivy leaves and sprig of rue, and position next to the cake.

Heavenly Scent Arrangement

This beautiful arrangement, taken from the Heavenly Scent cake on page 8, makes a useful alternative to a wired spray – giving the novice sugarcrafter a little more confidence as the flowers can easily be removed and re-arranged if a mistake is made first time round.

FLOWERS

3 stems of tuberoses (see page 12)
3 stems of ivy, plus some extras (see page 114)
1 full rose, 3 half roses and 5 rosebuds (see page 136)
2 stems of rue (right)

EQUIPMENT

Florists' staysoft
Small oval acrylic board (HP)
Wire cutters
Fine pliers

Preparation

1 Fix the florists' staysoft to the acrylic board (because this is only a small arrangement, the paste will adhere itself sufficiently to the acrylic).

2 Cut each of the tuberose stems to the required length, make a hook at the end of each of the stems for support and then arrange them in the staysoft.

Assembly

3 Start by positioning the three stems of tuberoses and ivy in the staysoft to form the basic outline of the arrangement. Curve any of the stems if necessary to form a pleasing shape.

4 Position the large rose at the centre of the arrangement to form the focal point, then arrange the half roses and buds around the central rose.

RUE

Rue (*Ruta graveolens*) has very pretty foliage. The leaves are made using two sizes of triple-spreading 'E' cutters (Zimbabwean cutters). Insert a short length of 30-gauge wire into almost the full length of each leaf. Work the edges using the broad end of the dresden tool and then cup the back of each section using a small celstick. Pinch a central vein down each one. Dust with dark green, holly/ivy and white petal dust. Dip into a ¼ glaze. Tape leaves into groups.

5 To complete, add the rue leaves and some ivy leaves to fill in the gaps and frame the focal flower.

TUBEROSE

The tuberose (*Polianthes tuberosa*) probably originates from Mexico, but it has been cultivated in southern France for centuries for the perfume industry. There are both single and double forms of tuberose, although the latter is the most popular as a cut flower. The fleshy flowers and chubby bud arrangement add a wonderful charm to sprays and bouquets.

STAMENS

1 There are three slender stamens in a tuberose flower – I use artistic licence using six stamens to add more interest. Bend three seed-head stamens in half and either glue or tape them on to a 24-gauge wire. Dust the tips with primrose and lemon petal dust. Attach a small piece of paste to the base of the stamens to help the first petals stick.

FIRST AND SECOND LAYERS OF PETALS

2 Roll out a small amount of white flower paste and cut out one flower shape using the smallest of the six-petal pointed blossom cutters (N3). Place the shape on to a pad and soften the edges using the rounded end of a celstick. Using the broad end of the dresden tool, hollow out the length of each of the petals. Using the fine end of the tool, mark a few fine veins on each petal.

3 Moisten the paste on the wire below the stamens with fresh egg white, then thread the wire through the centre of the petal shape. Pinch and form the petals around the stamens to form a tight centre (the stamens should be able to be viewed, but not standing proud). Work on several flowers at a time, so that when you have completed the first layers of all of the flowers, the first flower should be ready to have the second layer of petals attached.

MATERIALS

Small white seed-head stamens
18, 24 and 26-gauge wires
White and green flower paste
Primrose, lemon, vine green, moss green, plum, white and dark green petal dust (blossom tint)
¼ glaze (see page 151)

EQUIPMENT

Six-petal pointed blossom cutters (OP N1,2,3)
Dried corn on the cob husk
Leaf templates (see page 154)

4 Repeat steps two and three but this time use the larger six-petal cutter (N2). Attach to the first layer so that you have a petal positioned in between each on the previous layer. Make some of the centres tighter to represent newly open and fully open flowers. Dry slightly.

THIRD LAYER

5 Roll a ball of flower paste into a sausage shape and pinch out one end to form a pedestal shape. Place the flat part of the pedestal on a board and roll out the paste using a celstick, remembering that the tuberose has fleshy petals. Place the cutter (N1) down over the pedestal and cut out the petal shape.

6 Remove the flower from the cutter and place face down on to

the pad. Soften the edges of each of the petals, then turn the flower over and hollow out each of the petals on the upper side. Vein each petal as before.

7 Open up the centre using the pointed end of the celstick. Moisten the centre and then pull the first two layers on the wire through the centre of the flower, lining up the petals again so that each one is positioned as for the previous layer. Pinch the tips of the petals and curl some or all of them back slightly. Thin down the back of the flower if needed and remove the excess paste. Using a sharp scalpel, mark six lines as petal divisions on the back of the flower. Draw in some finer veins using the scalpel. Curve the back of the flower; firm up before dusting.

BUDS

8 Roll a ball of paste into a cone shape. Hook and moisten a 26-gauge wire and insert it into the base of the cone. Work the base of the cone down on to the wire to form the slender back. Using a cage with three 26-gauge wires, divide the surface to represent the outer petals of the bud. Pinch the tips of each of the sections to give them a subtle ridge. Vein the back of the bud as for the flower. Curve slightly. Repeat to make numerous buds of various sizes (sixteen buds pictured).

BRACTS

9 The buds and flowers are grouped in pairs down the stem and for each pair you will need to make a bract. They can be represented with floristry tape cut into a pointed shape, or preferably with paste. Roll out some pale green flower paste leaving a thick ridge down the centre (to give some support). Cut out a bract shape using a scalpel and one of the bract templates from page 154. Vein the surface of the paste using dried corn on the cob husk. Soften the edges and draw down a central vein on one side of the paste. Cut out as many bracts as you need and cover them with a plastic bag to prevent drying.

ASSEMBLY AND COLOURING

10 Tape two small buds on to the end of a ½-length of 18-gauge wire, using ½-width tape. Cut some strips of kitchen paper and wrap one around the stem and tape over. Remove a small bract from the plastic, moisten the inner part of the bract and attach to the stem at the base of the buds. Tape in the next two buds, thicken the stem with paper and again attach a bract. Continue, gradually introducing the flowers. Dry a little before colouring.

11 Dust the backs of each of the flowers and buds with vine green and then a touch of moss and primrose petal dust on top. Dust the tips of the smaller buds with these colours as well. Tinge the buds and add a streak of colour using a mixture of plum and white. Dust the bracts with vine, moss and dark green. Dry. Paint with ¼ glaze. Dry.

LEAVES

12 Roll out pale green paste, leaving a thick ridge down the centre. Cut out the leaf shape. Insert a moistened 26-gauge wire. Vein using the husk veiner. Soften the edges and draw down a central vein. Firm up a little. Dust and glaze as for the bracts, then tape on to the main stem, pressing the leaf base around the stem for a neat finish.

ORCHID INSPIRATION

The subtle colours used in the bouquets on this two-tiered cake are very fashionable with brides at the moment. I have combined phaius orchids, arum lilies, palm and other foliage to create a very fresh modern wedding cake design.

MATERIALS

20cm (8 in) and 30cm (12 in) teardrop-shaped cakes
Apricot glaze
2.25kg (4½lb) almond paste (marzipan)
Clear alcohol (kirsch or vodka)
3.25kg (6½lb) champagne sugarpaste
Fine pale coffee ribbon to trim cakes
Broad pale coffee ribbon to trim boards
A small amount of flower paste
Caramel paste colouring

EQUIPMENT

Sugarpaste smoothers
25cm (10 in) teardrop-shaped board and 40cm (16 in) oval cake board
Curved leaf and cornucopia cutters (ECC)
Tilting cake stand (CC)
Double-sided carpet tape
1 crystal pillar

FLOWERS

Orchid Inspiration Bouquet (see page 16)
1 small crescent-shaped spray (see page 17)

PREPARATION

1 Brush the cakes with apricot glaze and cover with almond paste. Leave to dry overnight. Moisten the surface of the almond paste with clear alcohol and cover with champagne sugarpaste, using sugarpaste smoothers to achieve a good finish. Cover the cake boards with champagne sugarpaste. Position the cakes on top, making sure you have a neat join between the bases of the cakes and the boards. Allow to dry overnight.

2 Attach a band of fine pale coffee ribbon around the base of each cake and a band of broad coffee ribbon to the edge of the cake boards.

SIDE DESIGN

3 Colour the flower paste with a touch of caramel paste colouring so that it matches the colour of the sugarpaste. Knead the paste to make it pliable and then roll it out quite thinly on to a non-stick board. Using the curved leaf and cornucopia cutters, cut out numerous shapes to decorate the sides.

4 Moisten the back of each of the shapes in turn with clear alcohol. Position them on to the cake surface, alternating the two shapes as shown in the main photograph.

ASSEMBLY

5 Place the tilting cake stand on the base board behind the indent of the large teardrop cake. Stick some double-sided carpet tape on the slope of the stand and position the smaller cake on top.

6 Assemble the bouquets as instructed on page 17. Insert the bouquet handle into a crystal pillar and then insert this into the top tier. (Do not position this too close to the edge of the cake.) Arrange the crescent-shaped spray on the right of the larger cake.

NOTE

If you are concerned that the top tier is too heavy to rest securely on the tilted stand, use a polystyrene dummy cake for the display and then provide a separate cake simply decorated for cutting.

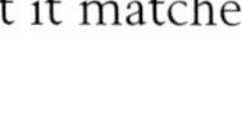

ORCHID INSPIRATION BOUQUET

Orchids have long been used as bridal flowers to give an exotic and extravagant feel to a wedding celebration. Here phaius orchids have been teamed with cream arum lilies, eucalyptus and palm to give a very modern, dramatic finish to the bouquet.

FLOWERS

For the large bouquet

3 Good-Luck palm leaves (see page 21)
3 stems of eucalyptus (see page 120)
5 phaius orchids (see page 18)
5 arum lilies (see page 36)
2 trailing stems of ivy, plus some extra medium and large leaves (see page 114)

For the small crescent-shaped spray

3 phaius orchids
3 arum lilies
2 stems of eucalyptus
3 stems of ivy

EQUIPMENT

18 and 20-gauge wires
Nile green floristry tape
Fine pliers
Wire cutters

PREPARATION

1 First of all strengthen any of the flower and foliage stems that will need extra support. To do this, tape 18 or 20-gauge wires (depending on the size of the piece) alongside the main stem.

ASSEMBLY

2 Decide how long you want the bouquet to be. The first palm leaf should measure at least two thirds the total length of the bouquet. Bend the stem to a 90 degree angle. Add the other two palm leaves, bending each of them to the same angle and taping them together with ½-width tape, to form the basic structure and a handle to the bouquet. Next, add the three stems of eucalyptus in between the palm.

3 Start to tape in the phaius orchids, using the largest one to form the focal point. (Remember this flower should be higher in the bouquet than any of the others.) Position each of the orchids so that they are all facing different directions, as there is nothing worse than having all their faces pointing straight ahead.

4 Add the arum lilies, curving their stems to form an attractive shape to the bouquet. You need to use three flowers at the base of the bouquet and two at the top – forming a lazy 's' shape.

5 Finally fill in the gaps with the single and trailing ivy leaves. Neaten the handle of the bouquet using full width tape.

6 This is quite a large bouquet to use on a cake, therefore use a crystal effect plastic pillar to hold it in position, as the normal sized posy pick is too small.

7 Make the small spray in a similar way to the large bouquet, but form into a crescent, to fit in with the shape of the cake.

PHAIUS ORCHID

The phaius orchid (*Phaius tankervilleae*) was one of the earliest tropical orchids brought back from China to feature in British collections. They can also be found in tropical Asia and Australia, growing in swampy areas. I bought this orchid as a cut flower (which is probably a hybrid form) from a well known department store; it was reduced in price and looking very sorry for itself – but it still cost me £8! Although this orchid is not generally used in bridal work, I thought its unusual colour combination made it a useful flower as this type of colour has been a very popular colour scheme with brides recently: it would work very well with the rose called Leonardis which has a similar colouring.

COLUMN

1 Tape over a short length of 20-gauge wire with ¼-width white floristry tape. Form a small ball of white flower paste into a teardrop shape. Moisten the end of the covered wire with egg white and insert into the fine end of the teardrop, so that the wire is inserted into at least half the length. Using the rounded end of a small cel-stick, hollow out the upper part of the column, pinching the back of the column to form a subtle ridge. To form the pollinia, add a tiny ball of paste to the front of the column and divide it into two using a scalpel. Allow to dry thoroughly.

THROAT PETAL (LABELLUM)

2 Roll out some white flower paste thinly, leaving the central area slightly thicker. Place the throat petal template on top of the paste and cut out using a sharp scalpel. Vein the upper surface using the amaryllis veiner.

3 Double frill the scalloped edges using the broad end of the dresden tool, then soften the frill using the ceramic silk veining tool or a cocktail stick (toothpick) to frill over the top.

4 Place the petal on to a pad and cup the two outer sections of the petal. Apply a little egg white to the 'V' shape at the base of the petal. Place the column on to

MATERIALS

White and pale green flower paste
18, 20, 24, 28 and 33-gauge wires
White, lemon, primrose, plum, aubergine, tangerine, skintone, red, brown, nutkin brown and vine green petal dust (blossom tint)
Deep magenta craft dust
Clear alcohol (vodka)

EQUIPMENT

White and nile green floristry tape
Phaius orchid templates (see page 154)
Sharp scalpel
Single amaryllis veiner (Asi-es)
All veined lily petal veiner (GI)
Ceramic silk veining tool (HP)
Dried corn on the cob husk

the left hand side of the petal shape, starting at the base of the column about 1cm (½in) away from the pointed base of the petal. Wrap the right hand side over the top to hide the column. Curl back the edge of the right hand side of the petal. You should have some excess paste at the base of the petal, which needs to be squeezed into a pointed shape and curled underneath the petal to form a spur. Divide this spur into two using a pair of small scissors. Allow to firm up a little before colouring the lip.

COLOURING

5 Dust the base of the petal, starting just above the spur with a mixture of white, lemon and primrose petal dust. If you are making a mature flower, increase the yellow colour and add some to the lip as well. Dust a small amount carefully deep into the throat. Dust a patch of plum and deep magenta craft dust in a curved shape on the lip. The more mature the flower is, the darker the colouring will be. If you want to make it very dark, mix a little aubergine with plum and deep magenta, and then dilute with a small amount of clear alcohol. Paint some lines into the throat using a fine paintbrush. If the end result is too extreme, simply dust over the top to blend the lines in with the base colour. Dust the edges of the throat with a tiny amount of colour if desired. Dust a very pale patch of the deep magenta and plum mixture on to the underside of the throat.

PETALS AND SEPALS

6 Roll out some white flower paste thinly using a large celstick, leaving the central part slightly thicker. (You may use a grooved board if you wish.) Place the petal template on top of the paste and cut out the petal using a sharp scalpel.

7 Insert a short length of moistened 28-gauge white wire into the thick ridge of the petal, holding the paste firmly between your finger and thumb to prevent the wire piercing through to the surface of the paste. Vein the petal using the double-sided all veined lily petal veiner, then place on a pad and soften the edges a little using the rounded end of a large celstick. Do not try to frill the paste as this will make the orchid look untidy. Pinch the base and the very tip of the petal between your finger and thumb. Repeat to make a pair of petals, one dorsal and two lateral sepals. Make sure that you keep them all covered to stop the surface of the paste drying out before you dust them.

COLOURING

8 The main problem with colouring the petals and sepals is that the backs of each of them should be white or creamy white and the upper surface a medium to dark reddish – brown. The only advice I can give is handle with care! Dust each petal/sepal in layers of tangerine, skintone, red and brown petal dust. The edges of each should be much paler. This colouring depends on the maturity of the flower and also the specific variety, and of course your own personal taste. To highlight the veins on the petals/sepals, brush a small amount of nutkin brown across the veins.

9 Allow each of the petals to semi-dry over a very gentle curve before assembling the flower.

10 Tape the narrow petals on to either side of the throat, using ½-width floristry tape. Next, tape in the dorsal and lateral sepals tightly behind the inner petals. While the paste is still pliable, re-shape the flower if needed. The stem from the back of the orchid to the main stem is a creamy colour, fleshy and has ridges on the back. I decided that this would make the flower difficult to arrange into sprays, so I have only

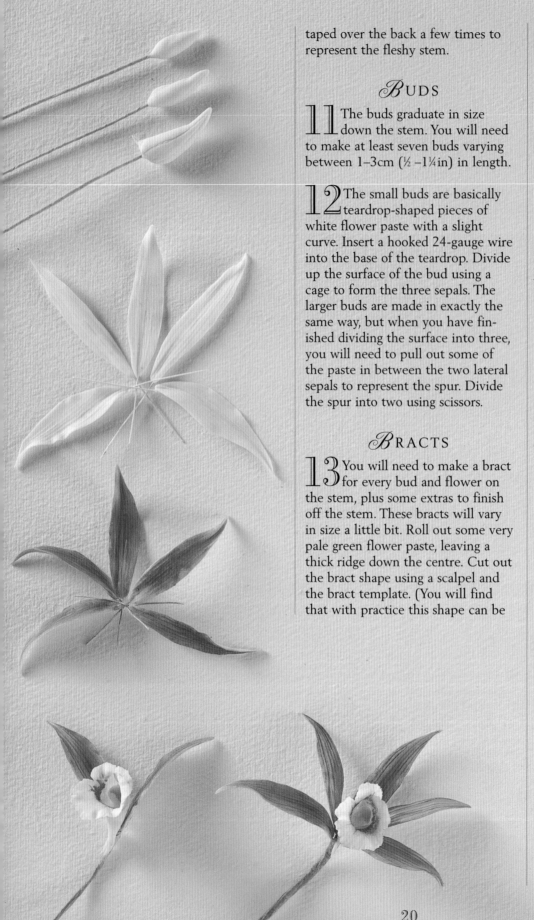

taped over the back a few times to represent the fleshy stem.

BUDS

11 The buds graduate in size down the stem. You will need to make at least seven buds varying between 1–3cm (½ –1¼in) in length.

12 The small buds are basically teardrop-shaped pieces of white flower paste with a slight curve. Insert a hooked 24-gauge wire into the base of the teardrop. Divide up the surface of the bud using a cage to form the three sepals. The larger buds are made in exactly the same way, but when you have finished dividing the surface into three, you will need to pull out some of the paste in between the two lateral sepals to represent the spur. Divide the spur into two using scissors.

BRACTS

13 You will need to make a bract for every bud and flower on the stem, plus some extras to finish off the stem. These bracts will vary in size a little bit. Roll out some very pale green flower paste, leaving a thick ridge down the centre. Cut out the bract shape using a scalpel and the bract template. (You will find that with practice this shape can be cut out freehand – or you might have a cutter in your workbox that is roughly the same shape.) Insert a moistened 28-gauge wire into the thick ridge so that it supports at least half the length of the bract. Using the length of a packet of 33-gauge wires or a piece of dried corn on the cob husk, vein both sides of the bract. Place on to a pad and soften the edges then, using the broad end of the dresden tool, hollow out the inner part of the bract. Pinch the length of the bract between your fingers and thumb, then allow to dry with a slight curve. Dust lightly with vine green petal dust.

ASSEMBLY

14 Start the orchid spike with a small bud and bract. Tape on to an 18-gauge wire using ½-width nile green floristry tape, leaving part of the bud stem showing. Continue to add the buds and bracts down the stem, keeping them quite close together to begin with, then gradually space them a little more as you start using the larger buds. When you have added all of the buds, tape in the flowers. Leave quite a reasonable length on each of the flower stems, but continue to tape the bracts tightly at the axil between the flower stem and the main stem. On one spike of phaius, there can be up to fifteen flowers (a combination of buds and flowers). Add a couple more lengths of 18-gauge wire to give the stem more bulk and strength. Continue to add the remaining bracts down the stem at intervals.

15 Dust the buds and the main stem with vine green petal dust; the smaller the bud, the greener it will be – but you must keep the colouring very subtle throughout. Bend the stem in shape and then steam to remove the dry dusted appearance. The leaves are very long and not suitable for use on cakes.

Good-Luck Palm

Palms provide a very bold foliage that instantly give an arrangement or bouquet a very exotic, dramatic and modern appearance. Good-Luck palm (*Chamaedrea elegans*), often known as the Parlour palm, originates from Mexico. Although it is not commonly used in bridal work, it is a good size for the flower maker to replicate in sugar and because of its common name it seemed appropriate for wedding cakes.

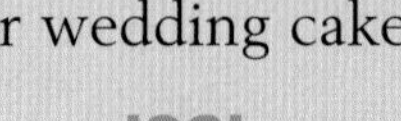

MATERIALS

Mid-green flower paste
20, 24 and 33-gauge wires
Aubergine, dark green and holly/ivy petal dust (blossom tint)
¼ or ½ glaze (see page 151)

EQUIPMENT

Leaf templates (see page 154) or fresh palm leaves
Long leaf cutters (TT665,666)
Sharp scalpel
Piece of sponge
Nile green floristry tape

Top Leaves

1 Roll out some mid-green flower paste, leaving a thick central ridge. Place the template or fresh palm on top of the paste and cut out the shape using a sharp scalpel. Insert a moistened 24-gauge wire into the thick ridge of the leaf. Use the fresh leaves to vein the paste if possible. Alternatively, press the length of a packet of 33-gauge wire on to the paste. Pinch the tips of the leaf, then place on a piece of sponge to firm up.

2 Repeat this process until you have cut out enough leaves to make a complete piece. Some of the leaf sizes can be cut out using the long leaf cutters, but this won't make all of the sizes.

Colouring

3 Dust the edges of each leaf with aubergine and then over-dust heavily with dark green and holly/ivy petal dust. Allow to dry. Dip into either a ¼ or ½ glaze, depending on your own taste, shake off excess and leave to dry.

Assembly

4 Tape the leaves on to a 20-gauge wire, alternating them from side to side. Add extra wire to support the weight and to add length to the palm. Dust the main stem with the holly/ivy and dark green petal dust and then bend the whole stem into shape using pliers.

Note

As these leaves are very fragile, make sure the wire is inserted into a good length of each leaf. Another method that is very useful for long leaves is to roll out a long piece of paste thinly on to a grooved board. Moisten the wire and lie it on the paste where the groove is to sandwich the wire and then fold over the excess paste, re-roll and cut out as normal. With this method, the wire will be running the whole length of the leaf.

It is also a very useful method for bluebell, daffodil and orchid leaves, and also useful for very reflexed lily petals.

AMERICAN-STYLE GERBERA WEDDING CAKE

Here, a very unusual combination of pink gerberas, bells of Ireland and red ink plant have been used in two informal sprays on a pink American-style tiered cake to create an attractive, bold and fun alternative wedding cake design.

MATERIALS

15cm (6 in), 20cm (8 in) and 25cm (10 in) oval cakes
Apricot glaze
2.5kg (4¾lb) almond paste (marzipan)
Clear alcohol (kirsch, cointreau or vodka)
3kg (5½lb) pale pink sugarpaste
Picot edge dusky pink ribbon
Pale cream royal icing

EQUIPMENT

15cm (6 in) and 20cm (8 in) thin oval boards
38cm (15 in) oval cake board
Sugarpaste smoothers
No. 42 piping tube (tip)
1 crystal pillar (cut down to size)

FLOWERS

For the large spray
3 gerberas, one larger than the others (see page 28)
3 stems of bells of Ireland (see page 89)
3 stems of red ink plant and foliage (see page 26)
3 stems of eucalyptus (see page 120)

For the small spray
1 gerbera
½ stem of bells of Ireland
2 stems of red ink plant and foliage
2 stems of eucalyptus

PREPARATION

1 Position the two smaller cakes on to the thin boards of the same size. Brush all the cakes with apricot glaze and cover with almond paste. Cover the largest tier without a board. Allow to dry overnight. Moisten the almond paste with clear alcohol and cover with pale pink sugarpaste (the thin cake boards will be hidden).

2 Cover the large cake board with pale pink sugarpaste and position the large cake on top. Use sugarpaste smoothers to neaten the join between the base of the cake and the board. Place the other two tiers on top of the base tier, again make sure that you have a neat join between each of the cakes.

3 Using pale cream coloured royal icing and a piping bag fitted with a no. 42 piping tube, pipe a shell border around the base of each of the cakes.

ASSEMBLY

4 Glue the pink ribbon to the large cake board edges. Cut a crystal pillar down to the depth of the middle tier. Wire up the flowers, berries and foliage into a spray (see page 25) and insert into the pillar. Insert the arrangement into the cake before the surface of the paste has dried. Wire up the smaller spray and position next to the base tier to form a balanced design.

NOTE

This type of stacked cake can be very heavy to transport. The cakes can be transported separately, then assembled and piped at the venue.

GERBERA TABLE ARRANGEMENT

This arrangement has been designed as a piece to decorate the top table at a wedding alongside the wedding cake; perhaps two arrangements could be made, one to sit at either end of the table. This would probably only be suitable for a close family wedding, as the flowers used are very time-consuming to make. Another idea is to use the flowers from the wedding cake, re-constructed into this arrangement, to keep as a memento of the wedding day.

FLOWERS

5 stems of red ink plant, with foliage (see page 26)
3 stems of bells of Ireland (see page 89)
3 gerberas, one larger than the others (see page 28)

EQUIPMENT

18-gauge wires
Florists' staysoft
Small black spherical vase
Pliers
Wire cutters

PREPARATION

1 First strengthen any of the flowers that need extra support by taping an 18-gauge wire alongside the flower stem. Place a clump of staysoft into the vase, pressing it firmly down to make sure that it is secure and also that the weight is even to support the arrangement.

ASSEMBLY

2 Start by arranging the stems of red ink plant in the staysoft to form the basic outline and height of the arrangement. (The height should be at least one and a half times the height of the vase.) Add the three stems of bells of Ireland, following the curves of the red ink plant.

3 Place the largest gerbera at the centre of the arrangement to form the focal point. Place the two gerberas one at either side of the large flower to form a line. At this stage it is best to stand back and look at the arrangement and perhaps add extra foliage, like the eucalyptus used on the cake, if required.

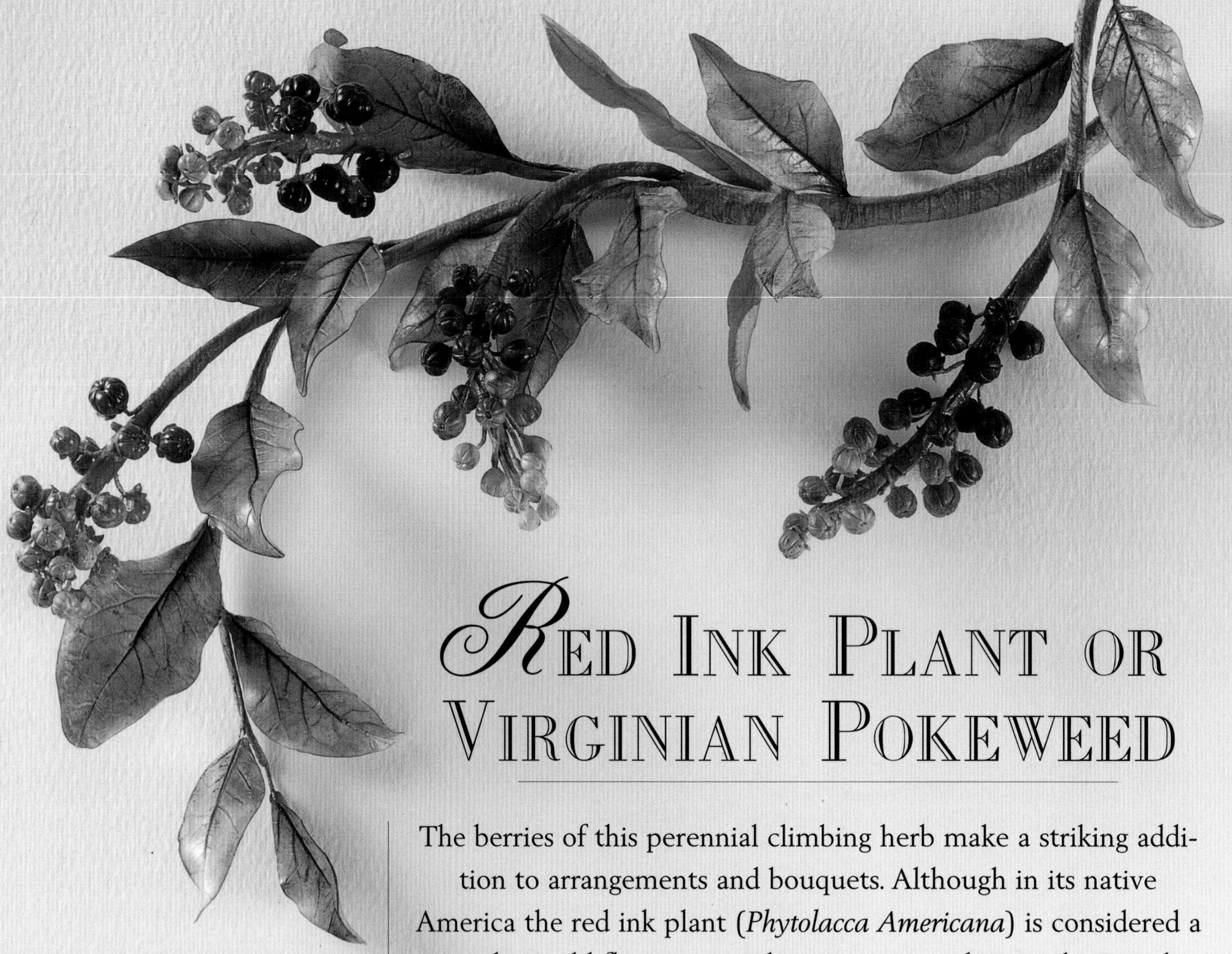

Red Ink Plant or Virginian Pokeweed

The berries of this perennial climbing herb make a striking addition to arrangements and bouquets. Although in its native America the red ink plant (*Phytolacca Americana*) is considered a weed or wild flower, it can be grown in gardens in the British Isles. The plant is poisonous, but despite this it has been used in the past to colour food and wines, and as a substitute for red ink. The berries start to form during the summer months and progressively turn into rich red-purple berries that have such a dark hue that they look black when fully ripened. They are available from florists from the end of July through to October.

MATERIALS

Pale green and ruby flower paste
18, 24, 26 and 30-gauge wires
Spring green, deep purple, black, moss green, dark green and aubergine petal dust (blossom tint)
Deep magenta craft dust
Full and ½ glaze (see page 151)

EQUIPMENT

Tiny Zimbabwean calyx cutter or small blossom cutter
Physalis leaf veiners (GI)
White and nile green floristry tape

Berries

1 Cut several short lengths of 30-gauge wire. Make a hook in the end of each of the wires. Roll small balls of pale green flower paste, graduating the size a little. Flatten the balls. Moisten the hooked wire and pull through the centre of each berry, so that the hook is embedded.

2 Using a sharp scalpel, mark deep striations, radiating them from the centre of the berry. Repeat the

process using the ruby coloured flower paste, but this time you will need to make the berries larger.

CALYX

3 The calyx is optional. You can either roll out some ruby paste, cut out the calyx using the cutter and stick it on the back. Or you can simply snip five sepals on the back of each berry with a small pair of sharp scissors.

LEAVES

4 Roll out some pale green flower paste on to a grooved board. Cut out the leaf shape free-hand or make a template and cut out with a sharp scalpel.

5 Insert either a 26-gauge or 24-gauge wire depending on the size of the leaf. Vein the leaf using the physalis leaf veiner. Place on a pad and soften the edges using the rounded end of a large celstick. Pinch the whole length of the leaf from behind to emphasize the central vein and to give some shape to the leaf. Pinch the tips a little more into shape. Allow to dry on a slight curve until they are at the leather hard stage before dusting. Tape over each of the stems with ½-width nile green tape.

COLOURING AND ASSEMBLY

6 Tape over each of the berry stems with ¼-width floristry tape. Tape the berries on to a 24-gauge wire to begin with, starting with the small green berries and graduating in size through to the ruby berries to form the fruit racemes. To thicken the stems as you work further down the fruit cluster, add a few more lengths of 24-gauge wire.

7 Dust the main stem and the short stems with deep magenta craft dust. Dust the small berries with spring green petal dust. Add a touch of deep magenta to some of the larger green berries and then dust the ruby berries to a bright pink. Finally, over-dust the large and medium sized berries with deep purple and lots of black. Dip the whole stem into full glaze, shake off the excess and leave to dry.

8 Dust the leaves with spring green, then moss, and a touch of dark green. Dust the edges with a mixture of deep magenta and aubergine. Brush some of this mixture into the central vein at the base of the leaf, tapering off towards the tip. Dip into a ½ glaze, shake off the excess and leave to dry.

9 To make a long trailing stem, tape the leaves, starting with a small one, on to an 18-gauge wire. Continue to tape in the leaves, graduating in size down the stem. Add a fruit raceme and tape in a leaf at the axil.

GERBERA

The ancestors of these cheerful cultivated daisies were native to South Africa – mainly the Transvaal and Cape Province, hence its common name the Transvaal daisy. The gerbera flowers (*Gerbera jamesonii*) can be single or double varieties and some of the newer cultivars have fringed petals. The spectacular colour range includes white, pink, red, yellow, orange and purple. Some gerberas have black eyes and others have green. When they are bought as a cut flower, they are sold without their leaves.

MATERIALS

18, 30 and 33-gauge white wires
White or pink, ruby and mid-holly/ivy flower paste
Small seed-head stamens
Aubergine, plum, dark green and holly/ivy petal dust (blossom tint)
Mimosa sugartex

EQUIPMENT

Sharp scalpel
Cymbidium orchid sepal cutters (TT20,23) or narrow daisy petal cutters (TT612,613,614)
Nile green floristry tape

CENTRE

1 Bend an 'L'-shaped hook in the end of an 18-gauge wire. Hold the hook halfway down with pliers and curl it back inside itself to form a coil. Bend the whole coil over so that it is at right angles to the wire and forms a ski-stick shape. Roll a ball of white or pink flower paste, moisten the hook on the wire and insert the hook into the ball. Flatten the top of the ball and pinch some of the paste down on to the wire.

2 Using a small pair of sharp curved scissors, snip around the centre to form lots of tiny hairs. Indent the centre using the rounded end of a celstick. Allow to dry.

3 Roll out a length of ruby flower paste quite thinly. Cut out a long rectangular shape using a sharp scalpel. Next, make lots of narrow cuts along one side of the rectangle so that it looks like a comb. Soften the edges a little by pressing each of the sections with the broad end of the dresden tool. Cut the tips off several seed-head stamens and cut the lengths to form lots of shorter strands. Moisten each of the strands with a little egg white. Attach along the cut side of the paste so that part of each of the stamens extends beyond the edge of the paste.

4 Moisten the base of the rectangle and wrap around the dried centre, overlapping the paste if necessary. Repeat this process three or four times, until the centre is large enough. Trim the stamens if they are a little too long. Allow to dry.

5 Dust the first part of the centre with aubergine petal dust, so that it is very dark. If the colour is not strong enough, steam and re-dust. Dust the outer parts of the centre with the colour of the finished flower. Paint the tips of the stamens with fresh egg white and dip them into some mimosa sugartex. Dry.

PETALS

6 The cutters used for this flower can either be the cymbidium orchid sepal cutters or narrow daisy petal cutters. Whichever you decide to use, they will need to be squashed into the correct shape. The cymbidium orchid cutters will need to be made narrower and the daisy petal cutters will need to be pulled out slightly to make them broader.

7 Roll out ruby flower paste, leaving a thick ridge down the centre. Cut out a petal using either of the cutters. Insert a moistened 30-gauge or 33-gauge wire, depending on the petal size you are working with.

8 Place the petal on a pad and soften the edges (do not frill). Hollow out the back of the petal using either the celstick or the broad end of the dresden tool. Turn the petal over and, using the fine end of the dresden tool, draw down a series of fine veins from the base to the tip of the petal. Pinch the base and the tip of the petal, then place to one side to firm up a little.

9 You will need to make a lot of petals to complete a flower – this will depend on how large your finished centre is and also if you are planning to make a double variety, in which case you will have to make a lot of small petals as well. I find it easier not to count the petals when I am making this type of flower. Do not allow the petals to dry totally before you assemble the flower. If they are drying out too quickly, cover them with a plastic bag to stop them being exposed to the air.

Colouring and Assembly

10 Dust each of the petals with your chosen colour. The underside of each of the petals should be much paler – I usually fade the colour out towards the tips on the upper side.

11 Tape the petals around the stamen centre using ½-width nile green tape, starting with the smaller petals (if using) and gradually adding the larger petals. Leave a little of the wire showing underneath the centre as this helps to give the flower more movement and longer petals.

12 Thicken the stem with the addition of a couple more 18-gauge wires and strips of absorbent kitchen paper wrapped around the stem. Tape over and rub the stem with the sides of a pair of scissors to smooth the tape out.

Calyx

13 Roll a ball of pale green flower paste into a cone shape, then hollow out the broad end using the rounded end of a celstick. Moisten the centre and thread on to the back of the flower. Remove any excess. The calyx is made up from lots of separate sepals. Roll numerous pointed strands of green paste. Flatten and vein the centre. Attach them over the base of the calyx so that they completely cover it. Pinch each of the sepals as you attach them to create a slight ridge on each one. Dust the calyx and the stem with a touch of dark green and lots of holly/ivy dust.

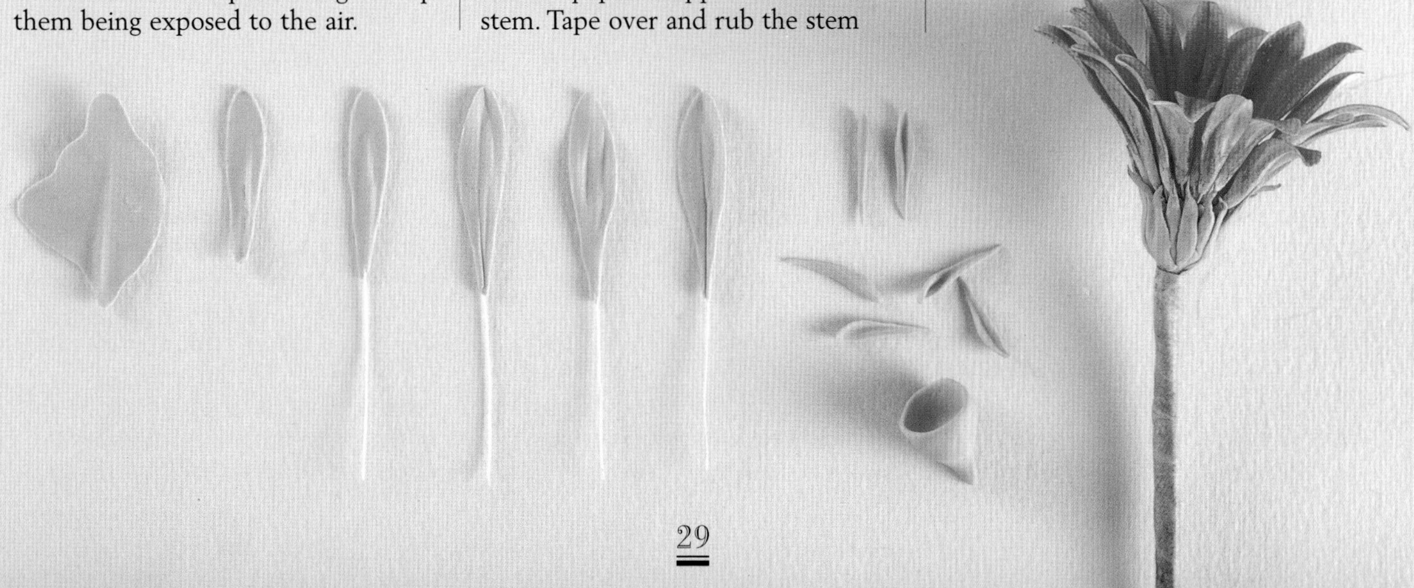

GERBERA 2

The alternative method used for this gerbera centre is slightly different to the one described on page 28. It is simpler to create and represents another type of gerbera. This method is not to be used for competition work as glue is not allowed to be used at all.

MATERIALS

Pale melon and holly/ivy flower paste
18 and 30-gauge white wires
White seed-head stamens
Primrose, lemon, moss green, apricot, dark green and holly/ivy petal dust (blossom tint)

EQUIPMENT

Hi-tack non-toxic craft glue
Cymbidium orchid sepal cutter (TT23) or narrow daisy petal cutter (TT613)
Nile green floristry tape
Glue gun and glue sticks (optional)

CENTRE

1 Repeat the first part of the centre as described in steps 1 and 2 on page 28. Allow to dry thoroughly.

2 Line up the tips of a complete bunch of small white seed-head stamens and hold them firmly between your finger and thumb. Using a cocktail stick (toothpick), spread some of the non-toxic glue over the length of the stamens on both sides. Blend the glue into the strands to bond them together. (Although it dries fast, this glue will not attach you to the stamens so do not worry.) Place the stamens to one side and allow the glue to set a little – if you allow the glue to dry completely, it will curl and buckle the stamens.

3 Cut the stamens in half, cutting across the length of the stamens. Now you can either glue the stamens with some more hi-tack glue or with some melted glue from a glue gun – I usually use the hi-tack, but you must be sure that the centre is completely dry otherwise you will just end up with a sticky mess. Wrap the stamens around the centre so that they are a little higher. Squeeze the stamens against the dried paste to secure the two materials firmly together. Allow to dry and then trim away the excess stamens. The finished centre should not be too deep as this will make the flower difficult to assemble.

4 Make the petals as described on page 28 and tape around the stamens.

5 Dust the very centre gently with a mixture of primrose and a touch of lemon petal dust. Mix together some moss green with more primrose petal dust and colour the centre gently. The outer part of the centre and the stamens need to be dusted with the flower colour. The stamens should be slightly darker than the colour of the petals. Add the calyx as on page 29.

NOTE

The gerberas used on the Floral Romance wedding cake on page 146 were made as a set flower, ie unwired petals. To make these flowers, cut out the petals in layers, using first a carnation cutter and then two sizes of sunflower cutter (TT669,673). Soften the petals and vein as described on page 29. Attach in layers, positioning the petals in between the previous layer.

PURE ELEGANCE

A very elegant two-tier off-set wedding cake with beautiful arum lilies, jasmine and ivy hand-tied bouquets. The delicate brush embroidery design on the sides of the cakes complements the floral sprays beautifully.

MATERIALS

20cm (8 in) and 30cm (12 in) kidney-shaped cakes
Apricot glaze
2kg (4lb) almond paste (marzipan)
Clear alcohol (kirsch or vodka)
3kg (6lb) white sugarpaste
White royal icing
Fine aqua ribbon to trim cakes
Broad aqua ribbon to trim boards
Holly/ivy, dark green, primrose and lemon petal dust (blossom tint)

EQUIPMENT

Sugarpaste smoothers
25cm (10 in) and 38cm (15 in) oval cake boards
Nos. 1 and 42 piping tubes (tips)
Brush embroidery templates (see page 155)
Paintbrush
Twisted silver-finish candlestick

FLOWERS

Arum Lily Hand-tied Bouquets (see page 34)

PREPARATION

1 Brush the cakes with apricot glaze and cover with almond paste. Allow to dry overnight. Moisten the almond paste with clear alcohol and cover with white sugarpaste, using sugarpaste smoothers to achieve a good smooth finish. Cover the cake boards with white sugarpaste. Place the cakes on top, making sure that they are central and that there is a neat join between the base of the cakes and the boards. Allow to dry for a few days.

2 Using white royal icing and a piping bag fitted with a no. 42 piping tube, pipe a shell border around the base of each cake. Attach a band of fine aqua ribbon around both of the cakes just above the shell border.

SIDE DECORATION

3 Trace the arum lily design templates on page 155 on to greaseproof (parchment) paper. Place the pattern on to the side of the cake and scribe the design on to the surface of the cake. Study the design carefully before you start piping – it is very easy to start piping and then realize that one part of the design should be tucked behind the flower that you are working on.

4 Using white royal icing and a piping bag fitted with a no. 1 tube, start piping a substantial line to outline part of a leaf or flower. Using the largest paintbrush that the design will take, moisten with water and brush the icing from the edge to the centre of the flower or central vein of a leaf using very firm strong brush strokes. Repeat to complete the design.

5 With a flower like an arum lily, pipe heavier along the lines that are at the forefront of the flower and again brush to soften the area where the edge joins the main body of the flower. Allow to dry.

6 Paint in the main colour and detail in each piece using petal dust mixed with a small amount of clear alcohol.

ASSEMBLY

7 Attach the broad aqua ribbon to the cake board edges using a non-toxic glue stick.

8 Tape together the two hand-tied bouquets (see page 35) and tie with broad white ribbon. Position on the top of the cakes.

9 Place the twisted candlestick at the back of the base tier and place the smaller cake on top.

NOTE

As arum lilies are a very popular flower for bridal bouquets at Eastertime, this beautiful wedding cake with an arum lily theme makes an ideal choice at this time of year.

ARUM LILY HAND-TIED BOUQUET

This style of bouquet has become very popular with brides over the last few years. The advantage of this type of fresh flower bouquet, rather than the traditional wired bouquet, is that the flowers can be placed straight back into water after the wedding ceremony. The hand-tied bouquet is very easy for the sugarcrafter to copy as long as you have sufficient flowers and foliage to complete the design.

FLOWERS

For the large bouquet
3 trailing stems of Chinese jasmine (see page 38)
7 arum lilies (see page 36)
1 long stem and two shorter stems of ivy (see page 114)
3 stems of eucalyptus (see page 120)

For the small bouquet
3 short stems of Chinese jasmine
5 arum lilies
3 stems of ivy
2 stems of trailing ivy
2 stems of eucalyptus

EQUIPMENT

18-gauge wires
Pliers
Wire cutters
Nile green floristry tape
Broad white silk ribbon

PREPARATION

1 First of all, strengthen any of the stems and foliage that may need some extra support, by taping in additional 18-gauge wires, making sure that each of the stems is neatly finished.

ASSEMBLY

2 Tape together at one point, a long trailing stem of jasmine, a small arum lily and a long stem of ivy using ½-width nile green floristry tape. A florist would usually tie the flowers together using raffia, ribbon or string – it is easier for the sugarcrafter to use tape.

3 Next tape in two arum lilies, slightly behind and one either side of the first one, with their points to either side of the bouquet. Tape in a long piece of eucalyptus underneath the arum lily on the right hand side (when you hold the bouquet to wire it together it will be on the left hand side). Again tape all of these pieces at one point.

4 Continue to add the arum lilies, alternating them from side to side in the bouquet. One of the larger flowers should be positioned a little more centrally than the others to form the focal point. As you work down the bouquet, continue to add jasmine stems, eucalyptus and ivy. When the bouquet has been completed, tape over the area where the last flowers join to neaten the finish. Trim the stems and then tie a silk ribbon into a bow with long trails to hide the floristry tape.

5 The smaller spray on the top of the cake is made in the same way as for the larger bouquet, creating a little more of a curve and some height at the top of the spray.

Arum Lily

To be correct this is not an arum or a lily, but it is commonly known as an Arum or Calla lily (*Zantedeschia*) by florists. They originate from Africa and have for a long time, since 1687, been cultivated in Europe. There are many varieties covering a colour range of white, yellow, pink, green, red, burgundy and almost black. The white varieties are most commonly used in bridal work, often thought to symbolize purity. My favourite forms have large spathes coloured with strong green streaks. Arum lilies, whatever the colour, give a bridal bouquet a very strong, modern, uncluttered appearance. The flower shown here is a copy of a medium sized creamy coloured flower that has a dark burgundy eye at the base of the spathe.

Spadix

1 Tape over a length of 18-gauge wire with ½-width nile green floristry tape, then moisten the end with a small amount of egg white. Roll a piece of white flower paste into a medium sized ball and insert the wire into it. Work the paste firmly and quickly between your fingers and thumb to cover about 4.5cm (1¾in) of the wire. Smooth the shape down between the palms of your hands, then remove any excess paste from the base. Attach another piece of paste at the base of the spadix to give the base of the flower more padding.

MATERIALS

White or pale bitter lemon and mid-green flower paste
18 and 20-gauge wires
Aubergine, white, moss green, primrose and dark green petal dust (blossom tint)
Mimosa yellow sugartex
¾ glaze or glaze in an aerosol can (see page 151)

EQUIPMENT

Nile green floristry tape
Arum lily templates (see page 155)
Extra large amaryllis veiner (GI)
Lords and ladies leaf cutter (TT604)
Arum lily leaf veiner (GI)

2 While the paste is still fresh, dust over the top of the spadix with aubergine petal dust. (This is only if you are trying to create this specific variety of arum lily. If you are making the more common white variety, dust with lemon petal dust.) Moisten

the surface of the spadix with fresh egg white and then roll in the mimosa yellow sugartex. Allow to dry.

SPATHE

3 Roll out some white or pale bitter lemon flower paste; not too finely as this is quite a fleshy flower. Place the arum lily template on top of the paste and cut around using a sharp scalpel. Place the spathe into the double-sided amaryllis veiner and press the two sides together firmly. Remove the paste from the veiner, place on a pad and soften the edges using a large celstick.

4 Using the fine end of a dresden tool, draw down a few central veins on the upper side of the spathe.

5 While the paste is still fresh, dust a patch of aubergine petal dust on to the upper surface as pictured. (As before, this will depend on the variety you are making – the more common white form does not have this colouring at the base.) Moisten the base of the spathe and place the spadix on either the left or the right hand side of the spathe. (This will depend on the variety and sometimes you can have two flowers of the same variety that wrap in opposite directions.) Gently roll the two together, being very careful not to get pollen on the surface of the spathe. Curl the edges back a little, especially the long edge that overlaps. Pinch the tip of the spathe to form a fine point. If you are working on a very large flower, it is best to hang the flower upside down until the paste is firm enough to rearrange. Remember, in a spray you will need to have some flowers wrapped tighter than others. Allow to firm up before dusting.

COLOURING

6 Dust the base and part of the back of the spathe with a mixture of white, primrose and moss green petal dust. Dust the tip carefully with this mixture as well. You can also add a touch to the centre of the flower. Steam gently to give a slightly waxy appearance.

7 To thicken the stem, cut some absorbent kitchen paper into strips and wrap around the wire, taping over the top with ½-width floristry tape. Dust with a mixture of primrose and a lot of moss green.

LEAVES

8 Tape over a piece of 20-gauge wire with ½-width tape. Repeat this several times leaving 4cm (1½in) untaped, so that the majority of the wire has more bulk.

9 Roll out some mid-green flower paste, leaving a thick ridge down the centre. Cut out a leaf using the lords and ladies leaf cutter. Insert the moistened wire into the thick ridge and place the leaf into the leaf veiner. Press the two sides together firmly. Remove the leaf, place on a pad and soften the edges. Allow to dry slightly before dusting.

COLOURING

10 Dust the leaf with dark green, then moss green. Dust the edges with a touch of aubergine. Allow to dry thoroughly. Glaze using a ¾ glaze, shake off excess and allow to dry. If you wish you can etch away the main and some of the finer veins using a scalpel.

CHINESE JASMINE

Chinese jasmine (*Jasminium polyanthum*) is a wonderful filler flower for the sugarcrafter; it is very simple to make and gives a very delicate finish to a spray or bouquet. Used with its slender foliage, trailing stems and groups of flowers and buds, a very unusual, elegant bouquet or arrangement can be made. Try using this plant as the main feature for a winter wedding cake. It makes the ideal starting flower for the inexperienced flower-maker.

MATERIALS

White and mid-holly/ivy flower paste
24, 28, 30 and 33-gauge white wires
Fine stamens (optional)
Moss, dark green, plum, pink and holly/ivy petal dust (blossom tint)
¼ glaze (see page 151)

EQUIPMENT

Small stephanotis cutter (TT568)
Simple leaf cutters (optional)
Nile green floristry tape

BUDS

1 I tend to use many more buds than flowers, as they have a softer, prettier appearance, and more importantly, they are quicker to make! Form a tiny ball of white flower paste into a cone shape, and insert a dry 33-gauge wire into the broad end. (There is no need to use egg white with such a small piece.) Hold the base of the bud between your finger and thumb, then gradually thin down the bud using a rubbing motion. Try to keep the tip of the bud very pointed.

FLOWER

2 Form a small ball of white flower paste into a teardrop shape. Pinch out the broad end between your fingers and thumbs to form a pedestal. Place the shape down on a board and roll out the paste finely using a small celstick. Place the stephanotis cutter over the thick part of the pedestal and cut out the flower. Rub your thumb over the cutter before removing the flower to make sure you have a clean cut to the edges of the petals.

3 Place the flower on a pad and, using the rounded end of the small celstick, soften the back of each petal, working half on the paste and half on the pad. Using the pointed end of the tool, open up the throat of the flower. Moisten the end of a 28-gauge wire and pull it through the flower, until the end is just hidden.

4 If you wish you may insert a fine stamen in the throat of the flower. Move the petals around a little to add some movement. The flower has such a very fine calyx that it is unnecessary to add one for general work; if anything, mix a little moss and dark green petal dust and dust at the base of each flower.

LEAVES

5 The leaves grow in groups of five, seven or nine, and the top leaf is always larger than the others. I use a quick method for these leaves when they are needed for wedding cakes, as you will need to make quite a few to make an impact. (In my last book I made the leaves using squashed simple leaf cutters, which gives a good effect but takes too long.)

6 Form a teardrop-shaped piece of mid green flower paste and insert a moistened 30 or 33-gauge wire. Place the teardrop on to the board and, using the flat side of any rubber veiner, flatten the leaf to make it finer and form the leaf shape. (This will take a little practice before you achieve the correct shape.)

7 Soften the edges of the leaf using a small celstick, then pinch the leaf firmly with your finger and thumb to form a central vein and make the leaf look more natural. Make lots of leaves to complete a full stem. Allow to firm a little before dusting.

COLOURING AND ASSEMBLY

8 Group the buds and flowers into mixed clusters, taping them together with ¼ width green floristry tape.

9 Dust the upper surfaces of the buds with plum or pink petal dust. The flowers have less colour on them, again only on the upper surface (it tends to be where they are exposed to the light). Dust a patch of moss and dark green at the base of the flowers and buds.

10 Tape together the leaves using ¼-width tape again, starting with the large one and then taping the others in pairs down the stem. Dust the upper surfaces heavily with dark green and then over-dust with moss or holly/ivy. Dip into a ¼ glaze, shake off the excess and leave to dry.

11 To form a climbing stem, tape over a 24-gauge wire with ½-width tape, and then tape the leaves on to it so that you have two groups coming out at either side of the stem. The flowers and buds always appear out of these leaf axils. Continue to build up the stem until it is the length you need.

MAGICAL

This exquisite three-tier wedding cake, with its masses of delicate sweet pea flowers, trailing stems and entwining tendrils, would delight any bride who wants a magical, almost fairytale-style wedding reception. The actual cake has been kept very simple in form, with only some abstract bumble bees and delicate shading to break up the surface.

MATERIALS

20cm (8 in), 25cm (10 in) and 30cm (12 in) elliptical-shaped cakes
Apricot glaze
3kg (6lb) almond paste (marzipan)
Clear alcohol (kirsch or vodka)
5kg (10lb) white sugarpaste
Fine pale pink ribbon to trim cakes
Lilac ribbon to trim board
Small amount flower paste
Plum, deep purple, pearl white and white petal dust (blossom tint)

EQUIPMENT

20cm (8 in), 25cm (10 in) and 40cm (16 in) elliptical-shaped cake boards
Sugarpaste smoothers
2 long crystal pillars
2 posy picks
Pliers
Wire cutters
Bumble bee cutter (HH)

FLOWERS

18 stems of sweet peas (see page 46)
Numerous stems of sweet pea foliage with tendrils

PREPARATION

1 Attach the two smaller cakes to cake boards of the same sizes with a little softened sugarpaste. Brush the three cakes with apricot glaze and cover with almond paste. Allow to dry overnight. Brush the cakes with clear alcohol and cover with white sugarpaste, then neaten with sugarpaste smoothers.

2 Cover the large cake board with white sugarpaste and transfer the large cake on top.

3 Attach a band of fine pink ribbon around the base of each of the cakes. Glue the lilac ribbon to the base cake board using a non-toxic glue stick.

ASSEMBLY

4 Place the middle tier, off set, on top of the base tier. Insert the two crystal pillars into the back of the middle tier. Position the top tier on top of the middle tier and rest it against the two pillars.

5 Arrange the sweet peas and foliage into the crystal pillars behind the top tier, trailing them over the top of the small cake and then down over the middle tier. Insert a couple of posy picks into the bottom tier and arrange the remaining sweet peas into them. Try to make the arrangements as wild and informal as possible.

6 Cut out several small bumble bees from flower paste using the bumble bee cutter. Stick in position using a little clear alcohol. Dust with plum and deep purple, diluted with pearl white and white petal dust. Shade the edges of the cake using a pale mixture of the petal dust.

Sweet Pea Candlestick and Napkin Ring

This elegant candle arrangement harmonizes beautifully with the Magical wedding cake: perhaps several arrangements could be made to decorate the wedding couple's and guests' tables. The pretty napkin ring decoration could also be used to carry the sweet pea fairytale theme throughout the reception.

FLOWERS FOR THE CANDLE ARRANGEMENT

1 stem of purple sweet peas (see page 46)
1 stem of pale pink sweet peas
1 stem of dark pink sweet peas
1 stem of sweet pea foliage with tendrils
3 stems of trailing Chinese jasmine (see page 38)

FLOWERS FOR THE NAPKIN RING

1 stem of purple sweet peas
1 stem of sweet pea foliage

EQUIPMENT

1 beeswax candle
1 candlestick
24-gauge wire
Nile green floristry tape
Pliers
1 napkin ring
1 napkin

Candle Arrangement

1 Position the candle on to the candlestick. Tape over several lengths of 24-gauge wire using ½-width nile green floristry tape.

2 Place the sweet pea foliage on to the candlestick and wrap the 24-gauge wire around both the stem and the stick. In turn, add the sweet pea flowers and foliage and jasmine, and fasten each with the 24-gauge wire. Bend the various pieces around so that they form an interesting shape around the candlestick. Be careful not to let the sugar flowers get too close to the flame!

Napkin Ring

1 Fold the napkin into a rectangle and then roll it into a cylindrical shape. Thread into the napkin ring.

2 Place the napkin and ring on to the plate, alongside the cutlery, and then attractively decorate with the sweet peas.

SWEET PEA GARLAND HEADDRESS

This garland is not intended as a practical suggestion – you can imagine what would happen if it rained! This is purely a practice piece for the sugarcrafter, although there is nothing to stop a bride wearing or carrying sugar flowers if she chooses to do so. At sugarcraft exhibitions there is a trend at the moment to include a headdress in both the competition classes and on branch tables. On one occasion, I produced a garland similar to this one, but using roses and agapanthus instead of sweet peas, and displayed it as part of the wedding cake design!

FLOWERS

10 stems of sweet peas (see page 46)
Lots of sweet pea foliage, with tendrils
20 stems of lily-of-the-valley (see page 54)

EQUIPMENT

1 glass head
18-gauge wires
Nile green floristry tape
Fine pliers
Wire cutters
Broad gold chiffon ribbon
A length of white chiffon

PREPARATION

1 Measure the circumference of the head. Make the basic frame on which the headdress will be built, using 18-gauge wires. The final length of the headdress should be 4cm (1½in) longer than the circumference of the head. Tape several lengths of wire together using ½-width nile green floristry tape, overlapping some of the wire in order to form a circle.

ASSEMBLY

2 Tape the sweet pea leaves and tendrils on to the frame at intervals using full-width tape. Next, tape in the lily-of-the-valley stems so that some of the stems point upwards and some downwards.

3 Carefully entwine the sweet pea stems around the frame to secure them into place. Continue to add sweet peas to bulk out the headdress, keeping the circle balanced.

4 Finally, add extra foliage and lily-of-the-valley to fill in any gaps. Tie a bow with trails at the back of the headdress. Arrange a length of white chiffon over the head. Place the garland on to the head and relax the flowers a little if required.

SWEET PEA

Sweet peas have to be one of the best loved flowers, with their instantly recognizable butterfly winged flowers, structured stems and clinging fine tendrils. They are usually taught as a beginner's flower. Here I have turned the traditional method for sweet peas on its head by wiring each of the petals which makes a much more realistic and less fragile flower. Although sweet peas can be used with other flowers, they tend to speak for themselves and so look best when used by themselves with their own foliage and wonderful tendrils. The sweet peas that I have copied have quite large, frilly petals and were based on a florist's cut flower; home grown sweet peas tend to have smaller flowers, shorter stems and much, much more scent. They were a joy to make!

MATERIALS

White and mid-green flower paste
20, 24, 28 and 30-gauge wires
Primrose, spring green, white, moss green, dark green, plum and deep purple petal dust (blossom tint)
¼ glaze (see page 151)

EQUIPMENT

Scalpel
Rose petal cutters (TT278,279,280)
Nile green floristry tape
Small rose calyx cutter (R13a)
Sweet pea cutters or templates (see page 156)
Ceramic silk veining tool (HP)
Fine pliers
Fresh sweet pea foliage or peony veiners

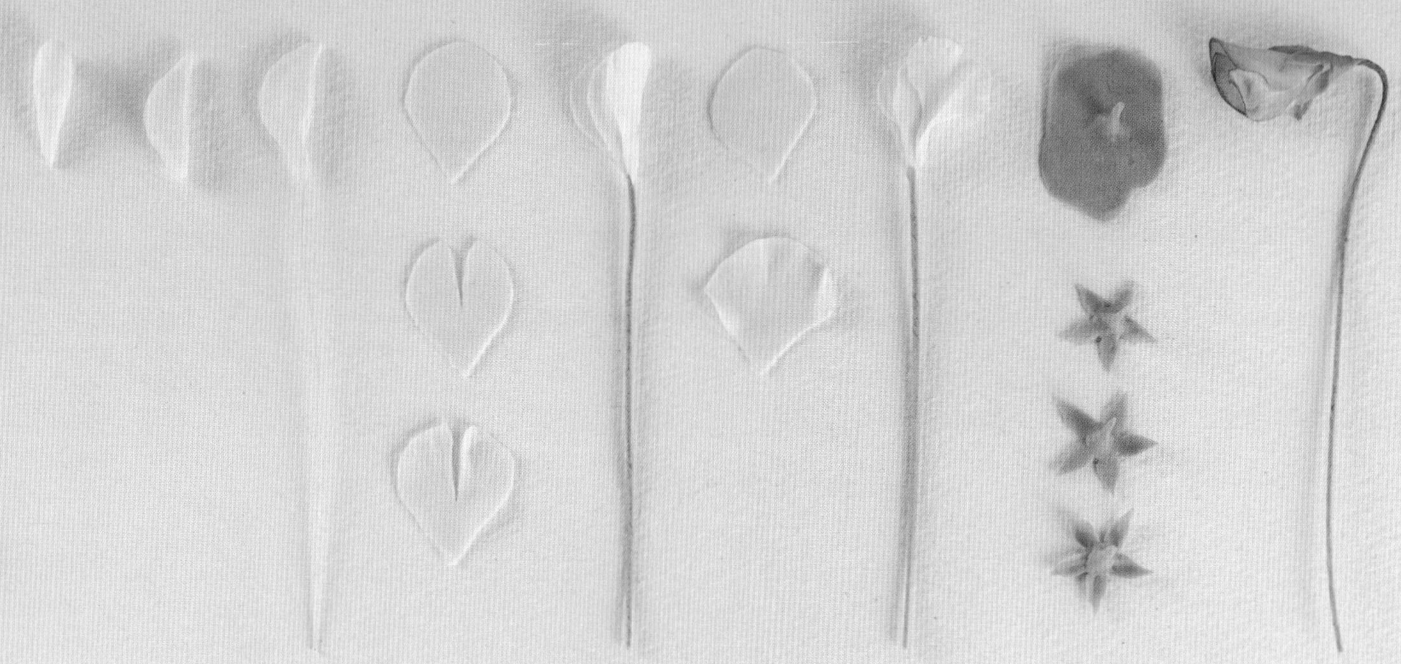

CENTRAL PETALS OR 'KEEL'

1 There are actually two petals fused together at the base that contain the stamens. This section is known as the 'keel'. In the past I have cut out petals to form this section, but in this version I create the keel as a solid piece, as it is quicker; also when the flower is assembled there is very little difference between the two. Roll a ball of white flower paste into a teardrop shape with a slight point at the rounded end as well. Flatten the shape with your fingers to form a pasty shape. Moisten a hooked 24-gauge wire and insert into the base of the shape. Pinch a sharp angle to the edge of the rounded part.

2 Using a sharp scalpel, indent and open up the straight edge to represent the opening for the stamens. Curve the straight edge back a little. You will need to make a keel for each of the flowers and buds.

BUDS

3 The keel for some of the smaller buds should obviously be smaller than those for the flowers. Roll out some white flower paste thinly and cut out two rose petal shapes using the cutters. Using a sharp scalpel, cut out a very narrow, deep 'V' shape. Frill the edges using the ceramic tool. Moisten the base of the petal and attach to the flat side of the keel.

4 Frill the second rose petal, draw down a central vein and stick on top of the split petal. Pinch the whole piece together at the base to secure and then curl back the outer petal a little.

CALYX

5 Form a ball of mid-green flower paste into a teardrop shape, then pinch out of the base to form a small pedestal shape. Place the shape, flat side down on to the board and thin out the paste using a small celstick. Cut out the calyx using the small rose calyx cutter. Elongate each of the sepals, by rolling them with the celstick. Place the calyx on a pad, flat side down and hollow out the centre of each of the sepals using the broad end of the dresden tool. Open up the centre of the calyx using the pointed end of a celstick. Moisten the centre and thread on to the back of the flower. Try to position two of the sepals on to the back of the outer petal shape. Pinch and curl the tips of the calyx back slightly.

6 Tape over the stem with ½-width nile green tape. To bend the stem, hold the point of the stem directly behind the calyx using fine pliers. Hold the wire at the end and bend this end over in a long swoop. This gives a neat curve to the stem.

FLOWER (WING PETALS)

7 Roll out a piece of white flower paste, leaving a slightly thicker area down the centre (this should measure only half the length of the wing petal and be very subtle). Cut out a wing petal using either the wing petal cutter or the template

from page 156 and a sharp scalpel.

8 Hook and moisten the end of a 30-gauge wire and insert it into the base of the thick area on the petal. Pinch the base to secure the petal.

9 Place the petal, ridge side up, back on to the board. Vein the surface of the paste using the silk veining tool, keeping the point of the tool to the point of the petal, working in a fan formation. You might also need to soften the frill, by rolling over with a cocktail stick (toothpick). Repeat the process so that you have left and right wing petals. Allow them to firm up a little – it does not matter about drying them on too much of a curve as they should be taped on to the keel well before they have had a chance to dry. They can be manipulated into the correct shape at a later stage.

STANDARD PETAL

10 Roll out some more paste, again leaving a thick ridge. Cut out the petal using either a cutter or the template for the standard petal on page 156. Insert a hooked 28-gauge white wire at the base of the petal (do not insert the wire too far).

11 Vein the petal and frill using the silk veining tool again. Place the petal on a pad and draw down a central vein on the upper side of the petal. Turn the petal over and, using the broad end of the dresden tool, hollow out two small indents, one either side of the central vein at the base of the petal (this in turn should create two raised areas on the front of the petal). Allow to firm up with a gentle curl.

ASSEMBLY AND COLOURING

12 Tape the two wing petals on to either side of the keel, using ¼-width nile green floristry tape. The long side of each petal should be uppermost. As the petals are still wet, you can now re-shape them to give a really good natural appearance.

13 Tape the standard petal tightly on to the back of the flower. Squeeze the base of the petals together to form a tight, neat join, then curl the standard petal back a little; the more mature the flower is, the further back this petal will be.

Allow to dry to the leather hard stage before dusting.

14 Mix a small amount of the primrose and spring green together with a touch of white petal dust. Dust the tip of the keel gently and in at the base of each of the petals. Dust the petals with your chosen colour, starting at the edge and working down towards the base. I used plum and white for the pale pink flowers, plum and a touch of deep purple for the darker pink flowers and deep purple mixed with a touch of plum dust for the purple flowers. Dust the back of the standard petals with a flush of the green mixture. Attach the calyx as for the bud. Dust the calyx with spring and moss green with a touch of white petal dust. Bend the stem as for the bud, but not so extreme.

LEAVES

15 When you buy sweet peas from the flower shop as a cut flower, they don't have their foliage with them. I have included them here, because I feel they set off the flowers to their best. Roll some mid-green flower paste, leaving a ridge down the centre (or use a grooved board). Place a leaf template or fresh leaf on top of the flower paste and cut out the leaf shape – with practice and for speed, you can cut these leaves out free-hand. Insert a moistened 28-gauge wire into the thick ridge. Vein preferably with a fresh leaf or with a suitable veiner. (The leaves in this step-by-step have been veined with fresh leaves, but the leaves on the Magical sweet pea cake have been veined using the peony veiner.)

16 The next step depends on the variety of sweet pea you are making, as some have frilly edges and others have flat edges. Frill partially with the broad end of the dresden tool and then over-frill with a cocktail stick (toothpick). Pinch the leaf to emphasize the central vein and then allow to firm up before dusting. You will need to make the leaves in pairs.

17 Dust to various degrees using dark green, white, moss and spring green petal dust. The leaves are not shiny, so you have the option of simply steaming them when they are dry or alternatively dipping them into a ¼ glaze. (The leaves pictured here were steamed and the leaves on the cake were glazed.)

BRACTS

18 At the base of each of the leaf stems, where they join the main stem, there are two bracts. These are very simple to make. Cut several short lengths of 30-gauge wire. Roll a small teardrop piece of mid-green paste. Insert the dry wire into the broad end of the teardrop and flatten using the smooth side of a rubber veiner (or something similar). Pinch the bract a little and dry.

TENDRILS

19 The tendrils grow from leaf stems (a common mistake is to tape them on to the flower stems). They just add character to the whole display. Use ¼-width nile green tape twisted back on itself to form fine strands. You will need three tendrils to form one group. Tape the three tendrils together on to a 24-gauge wire. Some tendril groups then go on to have another few tendrils below these three.

ASSEMBLY

20 Tape the flowers and buds into the stems with three or four flowers on them. Use a 20-gauge wire to form the main stem and leave a short length of each of the flower stems showing. The actual stems on a sweet pea are ridged – you do not need to worry about that sort of detail for cakes.

Lily-of-the-Valley Wedding Cake

Lily-of-the-valley has long been a traditional flower for bridal bouquets and wedding cakes, so it seemed appropriate to use these flowers on a royal-iced cake to give a formal, elegant design.

MATERIALS

15cm (6 in), 20cm (8 in) and 25cm (10 in) round cakes
Apricot glaze
2.5kg (5lb) almond paste (marzipan)
1.5kg (3lb) pale cream royal icing
Primrose, moss and white petal dust (blossom tint)
A small amount of clear alcohol (kirsch or vodka)
White royal icing (see page 152)
Picot edge cream ribbon to trim boards

EQUIPMENT

20cm (8 in), 25cm (10 in) and 38cm (15 in) round cake boards
Greaseproof (parchment) paper
No.1 and 0 piping tubes (tips)
Thick card
A4 plastic file pocket
Lace and embroidery design templates (see page 155)
Scriber
Crystal candle holder
Small and medium perspex dividers

FLOWERS

40 stems of lily-of-the-valley for the top arrangement (see page 54)
5 lily-of-the-valley leaves
9 stems of ivy (see page 114)
15 stems of lily-of-the-valley for the smaller groups
3 small stems of ivy

Preparation

1 Brush the cakes with apricot glaze and cover the tops with almond paste. Cut a long strip of almond paste and cover the sides of the cakes. Allow to dry thoroughly.

2 Coat the tops of the cakes and then the sides with at least three layers of royal icing until a smooth finish is obtained with a sharp, clean top edge. Attach each of the cakes to their boards with a little royal icing and allow to set. Coat the boards several times, then allow to dry.

3 Pipe a fine snail trail around the base of each of the cakes using royal icing and a piping bag fitted with a no. 1 tube. Glue a length of cream ribbon to the board edges.

Side Decoration

4 Trace the heart lace design on page 155 several times on to a piece of tracing paper. Cut a piece of thick card to a size that will slide into an A4 plastic file pocket. Insert the card along with the tracing paper into the pocket so that the design shows through the plastic.

5 Pipe over the lace design using white royal icing and a piping bag fitted with a no. 0 piping tube. Allow to dry.

6 Scribe a fine line on to the cake, either freehand or using a template, to help position the embroidery and lace. Using either a no.1 or 0 tube and white royal icing, pipe the lily-of-the-valley buds and flowers on to the cake. Allow to dry. Paint in the main and flower stems using a mixture of primrose, moss and white petal dust, diluted with a small amount of clear alcohol. Colour some of the smaller buds with this mixture as well. Finer detail can be added using a slightly darker mixture.

7 Attach the lace pieces to the cake with royal icing, piping two dots to hold each piece. In between each piece, pipe another dot. Follow the scribed line up to the top edge of the cake and then follow the edge of the cake until the scribed mark at the other side of the cake is reached.

Assembly

8 Make three small groups of lily-of-the-valley and tie them together using a stem of ivy. You will need one group of three, one of five and one with seven stems. Attach to the centre of the cake design at the base of each of the cakes.

9 Make a larger group of lily-of-the-valley and trailing ivy stems and insert into the candle holder.

10 Assemble the wedding cake using the perspex dividers instead of pillars. Position the cake top arrangement carefully on top of the small cake.

Lily-of-the-Valley Favours

Wedding favours can often be very fancy in appearance. If you want to give gifts that are more individual, try decorating small boxes filled with chocolates or sugared almonds with sugar flowers. The box pictured here is pretty but very simple, with only a few stems of lily-of-the-valley tied on to the box with a piece of dark green ribbon. On the opposite page is a variation on a theme. Here the guests may pick up their own almonds at their leisure from a plate decorated with a glass container of lily-of-the-valley.

FLOWERS FOR THE TABLE FAVOURS

40 stems of lily-of-the-valley (see page 54)
5 lily-of-the-valley leaves
9 stems of ivy (see page 114)
15 smaller stems of lily-of-the-valley and extra ivy leaves

EQUIPMENT

Crystal glass candle holder
Fine pliers
Wire cutters
30cm (12 in) round misted glass plate or dish
Good quality white sugared almonds

Assembly

1 Arrange the 40 stems of lily-of-the-valley, leaves and ivy into the crystal glass candle holder.

2 Place the arrangement on the centre of the glass plate. Empty out the almonds around it.

3 Place the smaller stems of lily-of-the-valley in sprays around the base of the plate at regular intervals.

Lily-of-the-Valley Favours Box

Line the favour box with some fine white or pale green tissue paper. Place some sugared almonds inside and wrap the paper over the top. Close the lid.

Tape together three stems of lily-of-the-valley and a short stem of ivy, using ½-width nile green floristry tape. Tie the lily-of-the-valley to the top of the box with dark green ribbon, then tie the ribbon into a bow to secure it in place.

LILY-OF-THE-VALLEY

Lily-of-the-valley (*Convallaria majalis*) flowers during May, but it is available at a price from the florist all year round for use in bridal headdresses and bouquets. There are both single and double forms, and also some with pink flowers! My favourite is the single white flowering variety. They are very useful for softening the edges of bouquets and look wonderful by themselves in tied bunches or small vases.

MATERIALS

24 and 33-gauge white wires
White and mid holly/ivy flower-paste
Primrose, moss and dark green petal dust (blossom tint)
Leaf templates (see page 155)
¼ glaze (see page 151)

EQUIPMENT

Tiny six petal blossom (OP) or five petal plunger cutter (PME)
Nile green floristry tape

FLOWERS

There are many methods to make lily-of-the-valley – I have tried most of them and I still prefer this quick method which produces very dainty flowers, fast! I have adapted an original method developed by my friend Tombi. I now use a very small six petal blossom cutter which wasn't available when she made her version. The method is based on an idea that Faberge used to create these wonderful flowers using flakes of mother of pearl attached to pearls to decorate eggs.

1 Cut several lengths of 33-gauge wire into 4cm (1½ inch) lengths. Bend a tiny hook on the end of each piece. Holding several pieces of wire at a time enables you to bend the hooks at a faster rate. I use 10-15 buds and flowers combined to complete a stem. I use any combination of the two as it depends what stage of flowering you are trying to achieve!

2 Roll a small ball of white flower paste. Roll out a small amount of paste thinly and cut out a flower shape. You will find that the paste sticks in the cutter. To remove it,

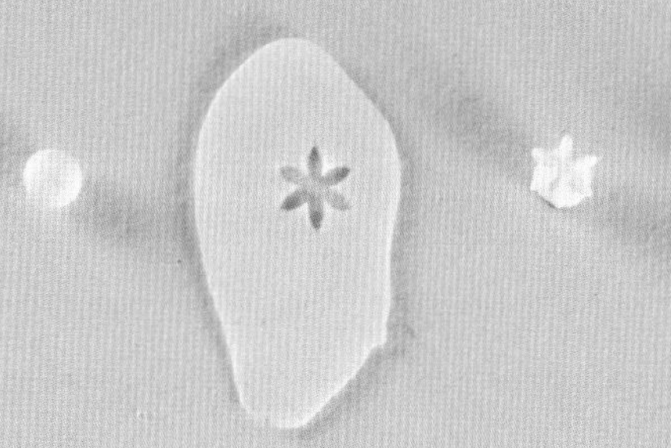

simply press it against the small ball of paste. Remove the cutter and the two should have formed a bond (you will not need to use any egg white for this.) Using the pointed end of a celstick, hollow out the centre of the flower. Press the sides of the flower against the stick to join the two pieces together securely. Moisten the hook on a wire and thread through the flower, embedding the hook into the sides of it. Repeat as many times to produce approximately 5-7 flowers for each stem.

BUDS

3 Make lots of small balls in graduating sizes. Insert a dry hooked wire into each one. Re-shape the balls to make them a definite round shape.

ASSEMBLY

4 Start with a tiny bud and tape on to a 24-gauge wire. Continue to tape in the buds, leaving a small amount of each of their stems showing. Alternate the buds and also use graduating sizes down the stem. Next add the flowers, again leaving a short stem on each. When you have added the last flower, bend each of the buds and flowers down using nipping motions with your pliers. Curve the whole stem.

5 Dust the main, bud and flower stems with a mixture of primrose and moss green petal dust, then dust the buds, gradually making them paler as they get closer to the flowers.

LEAVES

6 The leaves are also used by the florist, mainly because the plant is provided with its leaves and is very expensive. The leaves vary in their tone and depth of green and there are also some with variegated leaves.

7 Roll out a long strip of green paste on to a grooved board. Moisten a 24-gauge wire and lay it down the centre, over the groove. Pull back the paste above the wire and fold it over the top to sandwich the wire. Re-roll the paste to bond the two sides of paste together. Using the template from page 155, cut out the basic leaf shape using a scalpel. Remove the leaf from the groove and flatten the ridge.

8 Place the leaf back against the board and use a packet of 33-gauge wires to vein the length of the leaf. The veins should follow the curve of the edge of the leaf on both sides.

9 Place the leaf on to a pad and then soften the edges using the rounded end of a large celstick. Pinch the central vein and overlap the two edges at the base of the leaf. Allow the leaf to firm up before colouring.

10 Dust with dark green and moss petal dust. Dip into a ¼ glaze, shake off the excess and allow to dry.

MIDSUMMER WEDDING

A very striking colour combination of wild blue cornflowers and formal yellow roses has been used here to create a stunning summer wedding cake. The addition of honeysuckle and sprigs of rosemary help to marry the two very intense colours together.

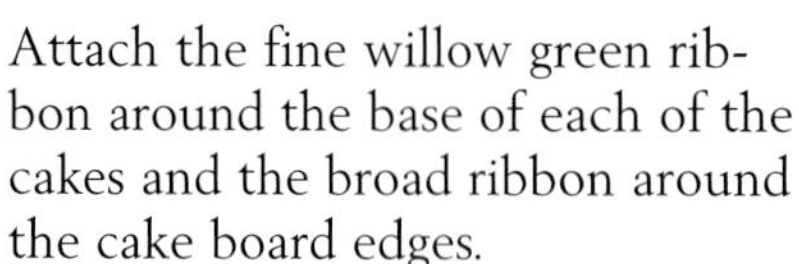

MATERIALS

15cm (6 in), 23cm (9 in) and 30cm (12 in) round cakes
Apricot glaze
3kg (6lb) almond paste (marzipan)
Clear alcohol (kirsch or vodka)
5kg (10lb) pale egg yellow sugarpaste
Fine willow green ribbon to trim cakes
Broad willow green ribbon to trim boards

EQUIPMENT

23cm (9 in) cake card
23cm (9 in) and 43cm (17 in) round cake boards
Sugarpaste smoothers
Antique finish candle holder
2 long tapered crystal pillars

FLOWERS

2 Midsummer Bridal Bouquets, one slightly larger (see page 58)

PREPARATION

1 Brush the cakes with apricot glaze and cover with almond paste. Allow to dry overnight. Attach the 23cm (9 in) cake to the cake card. Moisten the almond paste with alcohol, then cover the cakes and boards separately with pale yellow sugarpaste, using smoothers to obtain a good finish. Position the largest and smallest cakes on the boards, then place the 23cm (9 in) cake on top of the base tier, making sure that you have a neat join. Attach the fine willow green ribbon around the base of each of the cakes and the broad ribbon around the cake board edges.

2 Make two Midsummer Bridal Bouquets as described on page 58; the spray for the base tier should be slightly larger.

ASSEMBLY

3 Position the candle holder on to the centre of the middle tier of the cake. (Place a thin cake card, the same size as the base of the holder, underneath the holder to separate it from the sugarpaste, if preferred.) Place the top tier on to the candle holder, making sure that the whole display looks balanced.

4 Measure the length of the crystal pillars to the depth and angle at which they are to be inserted into the cakes, then cut them down to size using a hack saw. Wash the pillars in very hot water, dry and insert into the cakes. Position the sprays into the pillars. Using pliers, re-position any of the stems that have moved while being inserted into the cake.

MIDSUMMER BRIDAL BOUQUET

This bouquet adorns the base tier of the Midsummer Wedding cake on page 56. It was intentional to make this bouquet a little on the sparse side – I wanted to create a wild, country-style cake with space for the flowers and foliage to breathe. If a more structured bouquet is required, simply add plenty of trailing ivy stems. The top bouquet is a slightly smaller version of the bouquet described.

FLOWERS

4 stems of honeysuckle flowers (see page 62)
5 stems of honeysuckle foliage
6 sprigs of rosemary (see page 65)
1 full rose, 3 half roses and 3-4 rosebuds (see page 136)
5 cornflowers and 5 cornflower buds (see page 60)

EQUIPMENT

18-gauge wire
Nile green floristry tape
Fine pliers
Wire cutters

PREPARATION

1 First of all strengthen any of the flower stems, if necessary, by taping on an additional 18-gauge wire alongside the main stem.

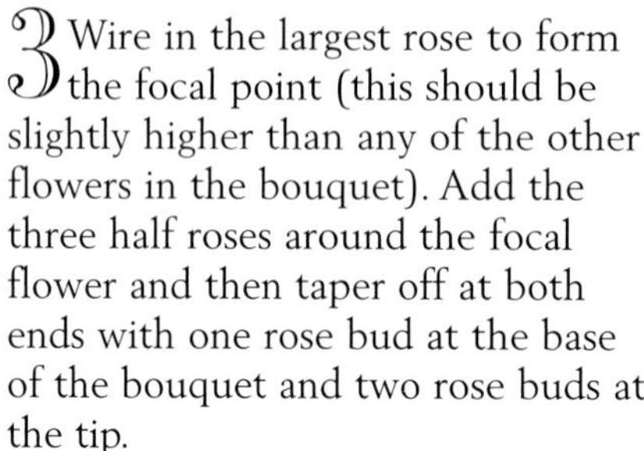

ASSEMBLY

2 Decide how long you want the finished bouquet to be. The first long stem of honeysuckle needs to measure at least two-thirds the total length of the bouquet. Bend the stem to a 90 degree angle. Next add another length of honeysuckle foliage, to form the remaining third of the bouquet. Bend its stem and tape in securely – the basic shape should now be an 'S' shape. Continue to add the remaining honeysuckle foliage and flower stems in the same way, along with the rosemary sprigs to form a complete outline of the bouquet shape.

3 Wire in the largest rose to form the focal point (this should be slightly higher than any of the other flowers in the bouquet). Add the three half roses around the focal flower and then taper off at both ends with one rose bud at the base of the bouquet and two rose buds at the tip.

4 Finally, thread and tape in the cornflowers and buds to complete the bouquet. Neaten the handle by taping over using full width floristry tape.

NOTE

Use a crystal effect pillar instead of a posy pick to hold this bouquet on the cake.

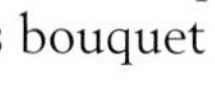

CORNFLOWER

The intense blue of the cornflower (*Centura cyanus*) is very hard to resist. There are some forms that provide white, pink and purple flowers, but it is the blue flowers that I am most fond of. They are very time-consuming to make, but the end result is very satisfying.

MATERIALS

Fine lace-makers' cotton thread
24, 28, 30 and 33-gauge white wires
Black seed-head stamens
Ultramarine craft dust
White and green flower paste
Deep purple, black, moss green, white, skintone, dark green and holly/ivy petal dust (blossom tint)
Cyclamen liquid food colouring

EQUIPMENT

Nile green floristry tape
Zimbabwean eight-petalled jasmine cutter

STAMENS

1 Wrap some white thread several times around two fingers to form a loop. Twist the loop into a figure of eight, then bend in half to form a smaller loop. Bend a short length of 28-gauge wire through the centre. Tape over the base of the thread and down on to the wire using ¼-width tape. To make two sets of stamens, bend another short length of wire through the opposite side of the stamens and tape over as before. Cut the thread in half to make two sets.

2 Trim the length of the stamens if they look too long. Tape in some black stamens around the thread centre and trim their seed-head tips off. Dust the thread with ultramarine craft dust, deep purple and a touch of black petal dust. Using tweezers, bend out the stamens and curl them. The centre of a fresh cornflower is actually much more complicated than this, but this is quite adequate.

FLORETS

3 I have tried several methods for making the florets and have found that by wiring each of them although time-consuming, produces a more realistic and less fragile flower. Form a small ball of white flower paste into a teardrop shape. Pinch out the base of the teardrop to form a pedestal shape. Place the pedestal on to the board, flat side down, and thin out the paste by rolling it with a small celstick. Place the eight-petalled jasmine cutter over the top and cut out the flower. (If you cannot obtain an eight-petalled jasmine cutter, try a six-petalled pointed blossom cutter.) Remove the floret gently from the cutter. Because it is so fine, this cutter has a tendency to pull off a few of the petals from time to time.

4 Place the floret back on to the board and elongate the petals a little using the celstick. Four of the petals at one side need to be elonated a little more than the others.

5 Open up the throat of the floret using the pointed end of a celstick, pressing the sides of the paste against the celstick to thin them out.

6 Place the floret on your finger, with the petals uppermost, and vein each of the petals down the centre with the fine end of the dresden tool. Pinch the tips of the petals and angle some of them back slightly. Bend a hook in the end of a short length of 33-gauge wire and moisten the end. Pull the wire through the centre of the floret, embedding the hook deep into the centre. You will need to make at least eight florets to make a complete flower. (This is based on the wild cornflower rather than a hybrid form which usually has many more florets.)

COLOURING AND ASSEMBLY

7 Dust each of the florets on the inside and the backs with ultramarine craft dust. Add depth to the centre of each one with a touch of deep purple. The more mature the flower is, the paler the blue it will be. Tape eight florets around the stamens, using ¼ -width nile green tape. Cut off the excess wire, leaving only a few, plus the 28-gauge wire from the stamens. The thick section at the top will be hidden under the calyx. Tape two or three 24-gauge wires on to the main stem to give support.

CALYX

8 Roll a ball of pale green flower paste into a cone shape, then hollow out the broad end using the rounded end of a small celstick. Moisten the centre and thread on to the back of the flower. Thin down the base of the calyx and trim off any excess. To form the scaled effect of the calyx, snip the individual scales using a small pair of curved scissors. Be very careful not to damage the florets as you do this.

9 Dust the calyx with a mixture of moss green and white petal dust. Dust a small amount of skintone petal dust at the top of the calyx at the base of the florets. To define the scales, mix a small amount of cyclamen liquid colouring with a tiny amount of black, then paint in the lines using a fine paintbrush.

BUDS

10 Wire a single floret on to a 24-gauge wire. Squash the floret up to make it look like an opening flower. Dust as for the flower and then add a smaller version of the calyx on the back.

LEAVES

11 Insert a 33-gauge or 30-gauge wire into a small sausage of pale green paste. Work the paste down the wire, forming a slight point at the tip. Place it down on the board and, using the flat side of a veiner (or similar object), flatten the paste to thin it out and form a leaf.

12 The leaves have slight serrations on the edges which can be made by flicking the edge of the leaves with a scalpel. Draw down a central vein and pinch the tip.

13 Dust with a touch of dark green and then over-dust with white and holly/ivy petal dust. Tape on to the bud and flower stems, then dust over the stems using the same colours. Steam the flower heads.

JAPANESE HONEYSUCKLE

There are over 180 different species of honeysuckle and many garden varieties. This form of honeysuckle has been naturalized in Britain where it flowers between July and September. Japanese honeysuckle (*Lonicera japonica*) is simpler to make as you do not need as many flowers and buds to create an impact compared with the more familiar honeysuckle where the flowers grow in clusters. They are easier and more effective to include in a bridal bouquet because of the trailing slender stems. The flowers can be white at first, becoming yellow later and occasionally tinged with a strong pink.

MATERIALS

Fine or small white seed-head stamens
20, 26 and 28-gauge white wires
Skintone, lemon, moss green, primrose, dark green, plum and aubergine petal dust (blossom tint)
Pale melon or white and mid-green flower paste
¼ glaze (see page 151)

EQUIPMENT

Nile green floristry tape
Glue gun and glue sticks
Honeysuckle cutters (OPHS1,2,3)
Simple leaf cutters (TT225-232)
Rose leaf veiner

STAMENS

1 The stamens in the flower are very small 'T' bar shaped anthers – these can be made in sugar, but they are very time-consuming. The following method has become a standard procedure where commercial stamens are used to represent the stamens, and the 'T' bar anthers are forgotten in favour of completing a wedding cake in time! Bend three stamens in half to form six. Pull one of the stamens so that it is a little longer than the others, for the pistil. Glue or tape the stamens on to a 26-gauge wire using ¼ -width nile green floristry tape.

2 Dust the tips of the stamens with a mixture of skintone and lemon petal dust. Dust the tip of the pistil with a touch of moss and primrose. Curl the stamens slightly.

FLOWER

3 Roll a small ball of pale melon flower paste into a long teardrop, then pinch out the base between your fingers and thumbs to form a pedestal. Using a celstick, roll out the base of the pedestal to make it much finer. Cut out the flower shape using the honeysuckle cutter.

4 Elongate the four upper petals by rolling them against the board with a small celstick. Roll the single long petal a little, trying not to elongate it as much as the other four as this will weaken the paste and make the flower too fragile. Pick up the flower and open up the throat using the pointed end of the celstick.

5 Rest the flower on the side of your finger and, using the broad end of a dresden tool, press several times on the central section of the four upper petals to give a slightly hollowed out appearance.

6 Moisten the base of the stamens and thread the wire through the centre of the flower. Thin down the back slightly and then bend it gently into either a lazy 'S' or 'C' shape. Do not mix the two shapes. Curl the long petal and the upper ones back.

7 Each flower has a tiny calyx at the base. This is made by attaching a small ball of paste at the base of the flower. Form the sepals by snipping several times with sharp scissors. Dust with moss green dust.

BUDS

8 Roll a ball of pale melon paste into a cone and insert a moistened 28-gauge wire into the broad end. Thin down the cone shape between your fingers and thumb, then bend it into the same shape as the flower back. Attach a calyx as before. Make the buds in pairs.

LEAVES

9 Roll out some mid-green flower paste on a grooved board. Cut out leaves in pairs of various sizes using the cutters. Insert a moistened 28-gauge wire into the thick ridge. Vein using a rose leaf veiner. Place on a pad and soften the edges. Pinch the back of each leaf from the tip to the base to reinforce the central vein. Dry the leaves on a curve.

10 Dust the leaves with moss and a little dark green. Glaze with a ¼ glaze, shake off excess and allow to dry. Add a touch of plum petal dust at the base, tapering into the central vein (see page 64).

COLOURING AND ASSEMBLY

11 Dust the underside and a little of the base on the upper surface of each bud and flower with a mixture of lemon and primrose. Colour the upper side of the buds and flowers with plum petal dust. The smaller buds should be paler. Dust the tips of the buds with a touch of aubergine petal dust.

12 Tape the buds and flowers into pairs and, if you have a lot of tiny leaves, tape two leaves at the base of each of the pairs.

13 To form a long stem, tape two small leaves on to the end of a 20-gauge wire using ½-width tape. Add the leaves in pairs, graduating the sizes. When the stem is started sufficiently, add the buds. Tape two pairs of buds, one either side of the main stem, and tape in a single leaf on both sides of the join. Graduate the size of the buds and leaves, then introduce the flowers in the same fashion. Bend the stem to shape.

14 Dust the main stem with moss green and over-dust with plum petal dust.

COMMON HONEYSUCKLE

Common honeysuckle (*Lonicera periclymenum*) is the form of honeysuckle that most people are familiar with. It has creamy-white flowers that mature to yellow, and can be tinged with apricot or plum or purple colouring. The flowers and leaves are made like the Japanese honeysuckle, then arranged into clusters.

LEAVES

1 The shape of the foliage depends on the exact variety of honeysuckle you are making; follow the instructions for the leaves on the Japanese honeysuckle (see page 63), inserting the wire into either the pointed or the rounded end as described. Dust and glaze as before.

COLOURING AND ASSEMBLY

2 Tape the buds in clusters of about ten, taping first the small buds together and then adding the larger ones. Add three to five flowers to each cluster.

3 It is easier to colour the flowers and buds at this stage as you can get a better balance of colour to the overall cluster. Dust the underside, then a little at the base of each bud and flower. Dust the upper sides of each bud and flower, starting at the tip with apricot, plum and then a touch of aubergine petal dust.

4 Tape two leaves below each bud and flower cluster, adding a 20-gauge wire if any of the flower clusters need extending.

5 To form a complete stem, tape the leaves in pairs, starting with two small leaves, on to a 20-gauge wire using ½-width tape. Add a bud cluster, then two leaves at the axil. Add the clusters, then gradually the flower clusters again, adding two leaves where the smaller stem joins the main stem. Dust the stems with moss green and the upper surface of the stems with plum petal dust.

MATERIALS

Small white seed-head stamens
20, 26 and 28-gauge white wires
Skintone, lemon, moss green, primrose, dark green, apricot, plum and aubergine petal dust (blossom tint)
Melon and mid-green flower paste
¼ glaze (see page 151)

EQUIPMENT

Nile green floristry tape
Honeysuckle cutters (OPHS1,2,3)
Simple leaf cutters (TT225-232)
Rose leaf veiner

ROSEMARY

Aromatic rosemary (*Rosemarinus officinalis*) is not only used in cooking, it is also popular with florists for use in wedding displays, bouquets and button holes. Traditionally it has been used to represent remembrance. The only problem with making this plant is that you need hundreds of very small narrow leaves to make a visual impact, which is why it is often ignored by the sugarcrafter if requested. If you decide to make rosemary, give yourself plenty of time. During the summer months rosemary produces pretty pale blue flowers, which could also be made if the plant is to be a main feature on a cake or of a design.

MATERIALS

Pale holly/ivy flower paste
22 and 33-gauge white wires
Dark green, holly/ivy, white and skintone petal dust (blossom tint)
Confectioners' glaze

EQUIPMENT

Nile green floristry tape
Small palette
Fine paintbrush
Any medium-sized veiner

1 I mentioned that this form of foliage is very time-consuming to make – that is true! It is also very repetitive and, I am tempted to say, boring. (My only suggestion to solve this problem if you are asked to make rosemary is to rent several good videos to watch as you are making them!) Although it sounds as if I dislike rosemary, I think the finished sugar foliage is wonderful and once I had finished making it for this book, I was very pleased with the end result.

2 Cut several lengths of 33-gauge white wire into fifths or sixths. Insert a moistened wire into a small sausage of pale green flower paste. Work the paste on to the wire and remove any excess length. Using a firm flat object (I usually use the back of a leaf veiner), flatten the paste against the board to form a leaf shape. If you have used too much paste the end result will be too thick and wide; to remedy this, simply trim off the excess paste with a pair of small scissors.

3 Pinch the leaf between your finger and thumb to form a central vein. Repeat the process many times until you have the amount that you need, remembering to graduate the sizes. Allow to dry.

4 Mix together a small amount of confectioners' glaze and green petal dusts in a palette to form a thick paint. Using a paintbrush, give only the upper surface of each leaf one coat. The smaller leaves should be a slightly fresher green to represent the new growth.

5 Tape the leaves in groups of two and three on to a 22-gauge wire until you have the length of stem you need. Dust the backs of the leaves with white petal dust and add patches of skintone on to the stem. When you have finished, breathe a sigh of relief!

Floral Rhapsody

Ranunculus make a wonderful alternative to the ever popular rose as a wedding flower. Here they have been used to create a cake that would be suitable for a small reception. The delicate embroidery complements the sprays of flowers perfectly to form a very fresh and pretty wedding cake design.

MATERIALS

23cm (9 in) heart-shaped cake
Apricot glaze
1kg (2lb) almond paste (marzipan)
Clear alcohol (kirsch or vodka)
1.5kg (3lb) champagne sugarpaste
Ivory royal icing (see page 152)
Fine orange ribbon to trim cake
Green velvet ribbon to trim board
Apricot, tangerine, red, holly/ivy and primrose petal dust (blossom tint)

EQUIPMENT

32cm (13 in) heart-shaped cake board
Nos. 0 and 42 piping tubes (tips)
Side design template (page 156)
Nile green floristry tape
2 posy picks

FLOWERS

9 sprigs of rosemary (see page 65)
3 stems of ivy, plus a few extra single leaves (see page 114)
9 ranunculus (mixed sizes) and 10 ranunculus buds (see page 72)
5 stems of rue (see page 11)

Preparation

1 Brush the cake with apricot glaze and cover with almond paste. Allow to dry overnight. Moisten the almond paste with clear alcohol and cover with champagne sugarpaste, using smoothers and the pad method (see page 153) to achieve a smooth finish. Cover the board with champagne sugarpaste and transfer the cake on top. Allow to dry.

2 Pipe a shell border around the base of the cake using a piping bag fitted with a no. 42 piping tube and ivory coloured royal icing. Attach a band of fine orange ribbon slightly above the shell border.

Side and Top Design

3 The side and top design can be piped directly on to the cake free-hand using a no. 0 piping tube or the design can be scribed on to the surface using the design on page 156 as a template. Once the embroidery has dried, petal dust with an apricot, tangerine and red mixture for the flowers and holly/ivy and primrose for the leaves.

Sprays

4 Use the rosemary and ivy to form the basic outline of the semi-crescent spray. Bend the stems at an angle of 90 degrees to create a handle. Tape together using ½-width nile green floristry tape. Cut off any excess wire.

5 Add the ranunculus, using the largest flower to form the focal point of the spray. Next add the buds and then the rue leaves to soften the overall appearance. Add a few extra ivy leaves to add depth to the centre spray.

6 Wire up a small straight spray using a small flower, a couple of buds and some mixed foliage.

7 Attach the green velvet ribbon to the cake board edge. Insert the sprays into posy picks, then into the cake.

Note

Inform the person who is to cut the cake that there are two posy picks in the cake.

FLORAL RHAPSODY TABLE ARRANGEMENT

This pretty arrangement has been created using the flowers from the Floral Rhapsody cake, with some roses added. Quite often the bride and groom like to keep the floral decorations from the wedding cake as a memento. To re-arrange the flowers into a suitable container gives a more permanent and decorative piece for the home. However, it is best to suggest that a glass or perspex case is made to protect the flowers from dust, and also that they are kept away from moisture and direct sunlight as food colours will fade eventually.

FLOWERS

8 sprigs of rosemary (see page 65)
5 stems of ivy, various lengths (see page 114)
5 short stems of rue leaves (see page 11)
9 ranunculus flowers of various sizes (see page 72)
9 ranunculus buds
5 half roses (see page 136)
5 rosebuds

EQUIPMENT

Florists' staysoft
Small verdigris effect container (or other suitable container or vase)
20-gauge wires
Nile green floristry tape
Fine pliers
Wire cutters

PREPARATION

1 Place a clump of staysoft in the base of the chosen container. Flatten the top of the staysoft. If any of the flower or foliage stems need strengthening or lengthening, tape in an extra 20-gauge wire alongside the main stem.

ASSEMBLY

2 Start by forming the outline of the arrangement using the sprigs of rosemary. You will need to make the height of the arrangement at least one and a half times higher than the container. To give the arrangement some depth, add the stems of ivy and the rue leaves.

3 Add the largest ranunculus flower next to form the focal point. Continue to add the ranunculus flowers evenly positioned around the focal flower. Try to position each of the flowers so that they face different directions. Add the ranunculus buds to the outer parts of the arrangement.

4 Last of all, add the roses, starting with the half roses which should be positioned deep into the arrangement around the large ranunculus. Fill in any gaps with extra ivy or rue leaves. Once the arrangement is complete, stand back and take an overall look at the position of the flowers and, if needed, move or relax them a little.

RANUNCULUS KNIFE SPRAY

I often have flowers left over when I am working on a wedding cake and these can be used to make a small spray to decorate the wedding cake knife. This spray can be just a collection of flowers and foliage or a single flower, such as a rose or an orchid. They are generally only used as a decorative item for the cake cutting ceremony photograph.

FLOWERS

1 large, 1 medium and 1 small ranunculus flowers (see page 72)
3 ranunculus buds
2 small stems of jasmine, with foliage (see page 38)
1 stem of rosemary (see page 65)
2 stems of ivy (see page 114)
1 sprig of rue (see page 11)

EQUIPMENT

1 cake knife
20, 22 and 24-gauge wires
Nile green floristry tape
Pliers
Wire cutters
Ivory silk ribbon

PREPARATION

1 Clean and polish the cake knife. Lengthen any of the flower stems, if necessary, with 20-gauge or 22-gauge wire.

THE SPRAY

2 Start the spray by taping together the three ranunculus buds with nile green floristry tape. Next, add a group of jasmine with foliage, then add the small ranunculus flower, using ½-width floristry tape.

3 Add and tape in the stem of rosemary and the longer of the two stems of ivy. Trim off any excess wire from the handle and tape over the top. Next add the medium ranunculus, then the large one, accompanied by a group of jasmine and rue leaves. Last of all, add the second stem of ivy, which should curve away from the front of the spray. Trim off the excess wire and tape over to neaten the handle.

ASSEMBLY

4 Take a couple of lengths of 24-gauge wire and thread them through the main body of the knife spray. Position the spray over the cake knife and bind the wire around the cake knife handle. You will need to bind the wire around the knife two or three times to secure it in place. Twist the remainder of the wire together to tighten the whole piece, then cut off the excess wire.

5 Tie a ribbon bow with trails around the knife and the spray to hide the join. Trim the ribbon ends to sharp angles using a pair of large scissors. Place the decorated knife next to the wedding cake ready for the cake cutting ceremony.

NOTE

You can buy small perspex and wooden stands to hold the knife in position if required.

RANUNCULUS

The genus name derives from the Latin *Rana*, meaning frog, which refers to the swampy places where these flowers are found in the wild. Ranunculus (*Ranunculus asiaticus*) have often been referred to as the up-market buttercup, sometimes known as the Persian buttercup; they are in fact from the same family. They are one of the most cheerful, colourful flowers and yet, at the same time, have a delicacy because of the fine petals. They are available for most of the year from the flower shop, but are at their best during the spring months which is when they are in season. Ranunculus come in all shades of pink, red, orange, yellow, peach, burgundy, purple and white; the size of both the flower heads and stems also varies. The flower shown here is a smaller flower.

CENTRE

1 Tape over a ½-length of 20-gauge wire with ½-width nile green floristry tape and bend an open hook in one end. Roll a ball of poppy (or your chosen colour) coloured flower paste, moisten the hook and insert it into the base of the paste. Flatten the top of the ball and pinch the paste down on to the wire to secure it in place.

2 Using a sharp scalpel, mark the surface of the paste to represent the inner petals, working from the centre to the edges. You will need to work quickly before the paste dries and the surface starts to crack. Indent the centre a little more by increasing the pressure when you cut the inner petals. Allow to dry.

MATERIALS

Poppy and pale green flower paste
20, 24 and 26-gauge wires
Primrose, moss green, apricot, tangerine, red and dark green petal dust (blossom tint)
¼ glaze (see page 151)

EQUIPMENT

Nile green floristry tape
Sharp scalpel
Australian rose petal cutters (TT351,350,349)
Ceramic silk veining tool (HP)
Nasturtium calyx cutters (448,661)
Leaf templates (see page 156)
Veining tool (PME)

PETALS

3 Roll out some poppy coloured flower paste not too thinly at first, as you will need a little bit of

thickness to allow the petals to be veined. Cut out many petals using the smallest of the Australian rose petal cutters (351). I cannot tell you how many petals to cut out, as it depends on the size of the flower you are planning to make and on the size of the prepared centre. If you look at a bunch of ranunculus flowers, each one seems to have a different number of petals. It is therefore best to start by cutting out six or seven petals, attaching them to the centre and deciding whether to attach more or stop and use the next size. (There are too many petals on a fresh flower to try and copy exactly, so all you are doing is creating an impression.)

4 Vein and, at the same time, broaden each of the petals using the ceramic silk veining tool. Roll the tool across the petal in a fan formation, applying quite a lot of pressure. Place each of the petals on a pad and soften the edges. Moisten the base of the petals and start attaching them to the dried centre. Some of the petals interlink and some do not on one flower.

5 Repeat the above process with the two larger rose petal cutters, adding the petals and stopping only when you feel the flower looks finished. Remember you will need to make some of the flowers so that they look as if they are only just forming. As you apply some of the larger petals, try to pinch them into place to create a slightly cupped appearance. Allow to firm up before colouring.

COLOURING

6 Dust the tight centre of the flower with a mixture of primrose and moss green petal dust. Then colour the petals using your chosen colours – in this case I have used apricot, tangerine and red. The back of each of the petals should be paler than the upper surface. You will need to make the petals closer to the centre slightly darker, so increase the red petal dust. If you are trying to achieve a very concentrated colour, steam the flower and re-dust. Steam the flower again to completely remove the dusted appearance.

CALYX

7 Roll out a small piece of pale green flower paste not too thinly, leaving a thicker raised section at the centre. Cut out the calyx using either the small or large nasturtium calyx cutters, depending on the size of the finished flower. Place on a pad, soften the edges and hollow out the length of each of the sepals. Moisten the centre and thread on to the back of the flower, trying to position each sepal so that they cover a join between two petals. The sepals should curve back with their tips curling towards the petals. Pinch the tips of each of the sepals into a point. Dust with a mixture of moss and primrose petal dust. Thicken the stem with shredded absorbent kitchen paper and tape over the top with ½-width nile green tape.

LEAVES

8 Roll out some pale green flower paste, leaving a thick ridge down the centre. Place a leaf template on top and cut out with a sharp scalpel. Insert a moistened 26-gauge or 24-gauge wire into the thick ridge, depending on the size of the leaf. Place the leaf on a pad and soften the edges. Using the veining tool, draw some fine veins on the surface of the leaf. Pinch the leaf down the centre and curl some of the ends back a little. Allow to firm up before dusting.

9 Dust the tips of the leaf with a little red petal dust. Using moss green and dark green petal dust, dust the leaf from the edge down on to the main section of the leaf, fading out the colour as you get to about two thirds from the tip. Dust the whole leaf with a mixture of moss and primrose petal dust. Dip into a ¼ glaze, shake off the excess and allow to dry.

MEDIEVAL WINTER WEDDING

The rich red amaryllis, roses and red-tinged hypericum berries combined with the ivy, dark green dusted boards and the red, gold and green braiding, make this cake a perfect centrepiece for a medieval-style December wedding.

MATERIALS

20cm (8 in) and 30cm (12 in) teardrop-shaped cakes
Apricot glaze
2kg (4lb) almond paste (marzipan)
Clear alcohol (kirsch or vodka)
750g (1½lb) sugarpaste, coloured with holly/ivy paste colouring
2.25kg (4½lb) sugarpaste, coloured with autumn leaf paste colouring
Red, gold and green braid to trim cakes
Green velvet ribbon to trim boards
Holly/ivy and dark green petal dust (blossom tint)

EQUIPMENT

25cm (10 in) and 40cm (16 in) teardrop-shaped cake boards
Broad flat paintbrush
Sugarpaste smoothers
Tilting cake stand
Double-sided carpet tape
1 crystal pillar
Pliers

FLOWERS

Medieval Winter Wedding Curved Bouquet (see page 77)
A few extra stems of large dark green ivy (see page 114)

PREPARATION

1 Cover both cake boards with holly/ivy sugarpaste. Allow to dry overnight. Dust the surface of the paste with a broad, flat paintbrush using holly/ivy and dark green petal dusts (the finished result should be streaky).

2 Brush the cakes with apricot glaze and cover with almond paste. Allow to dry overnight. Moisten the surface of the almond paste with clear alcohol and cover with autumn leaf coloured sugarpaste, using smoothers to achieve a good finish. Transfer the cakes to the boards, making sure that there is a neat join between the base of the cakes and the boards. Attach a band of braid around the base of both of the cakes using a small amount of green icing to hold them in place. Glue the green velvet ribbon to the cake board edges using a non-toxic glue stick.

3 Make the Medieval Winter Wedding Curved Bouquet as described on page 77.

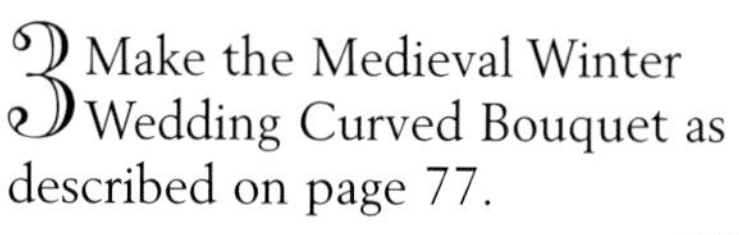

ASSEMBLY

4 Position the small cake on to the tilting cake stand using double-sided carpet tape to hold it in place. Place the larger cake next to the small one so that the shapes fit neatly together. Insert the long crystal pillar into the base tier and place the handle of the curved bouquet into it. Using pliers, re-position any of the pieces that need adjusting. Add a few extra stems of ivy to frame the edge of the top tier.

NOTE

If you are concerned that the top tier might slide off the stand, decorate a polystyrene dummy for the wedding display and provide a simply decorated cutting cake which can be kept behind the scenes.

MEDIEVAL WINTER WEDDING CURVED BOUQUET

The curved shower bouquet is my favourite shape for a bridal bouquet as it lends itself very easily to cakes. This style of bouquet can curve either to the left or right, but one side of the bouquet must be slightly heavier with flowers and foliage.

FLOWERS

1 long stem and 6 shorter stems of large trailing ivy (see page 114)
3 stems of hypericum berries (see page 78)
3 small amaryllis (see page 80)
3 rosebuds and 3 half roses (see page 136)

EQUIPMENT

18-gauge wires
Nile green floristry tape
Fine pliers
Wire cutters

PREPARATION

1 First of all, strengthen any of the stems that are to be very long or that are particularly heavy, by taping in additional 18-gauge wires.

ASSEMBLY

2 Decide how long you want the bouquet to be in length. The first long stem of ivy needs to measure at least two-thirds the total length of the bouquet. Bend the stem to a 90 degree angle. Add the other shorter stems of ivy, bending each to the same angle and taping in each piece with full width nile green floristry tape. You will also need to decide which way the bouquet is to curve and make the appropriate side slightly heavier. Add the hypericum berries next, making sure they are evenly spaced. This should form the basic outline of the bouquet.

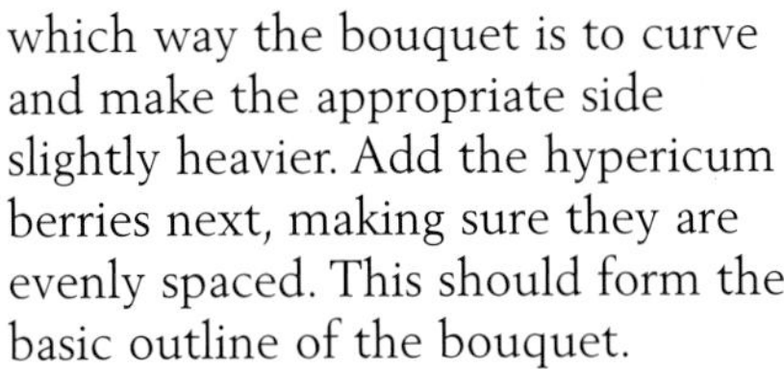

3 Next, tape in the three amaryllis, starting with the largest flower at the focal point (this should be positioned slightly higher than any of the other flowers). The three amaryllis should form a diagonal line in the bouquet.

4 Finally, tape in the roses to fill in the gaps in the bouquet. Cut off the excess wire from the handle, then neaten by taping over the top with full width tape.

HYPERICUM

Hypericum produces yellow five-petalled flowers with masses of golden yellow stamens. However, it is the fruit that is mainly used as a filler in bouquets and arrangements. There are many varieties of hypericum, each producing berries of a different size, slightly different shape and variations in the colour of the fully ripened fruit. They are available for most of the year as a cut flower from florists' shops.

MATERIALS

18, 26 and 28-gauge wires
Pale green flower paste
Moss green, primrose, red, aubergine and dark green petal dust (blossom tint)
Full and ½ glaze (see page 151)

EQUIPMENT

Sharp scalpel
Nile green floristry tape
Medium and small stephanotis cutters (TT56,568)
Leaf template (see page 158) or fresh hypericum leaves

BERRIES

1 Cut a length of 28-gauge wire into four. Take a small piece of pale green flower paste and roll it into a ball, then into an egg shape. Moisten the end of a piece of wire and insert it into the base of the shape, so that it almost pierces through the tip. Squeeze the paste between your fingers and thumb to form a fruit with three sides. Pinch the tip of the fruit into a sharp point.

2 Using a sharp scalpel, mark very fine striations on to the surface of the fruit. Repeat the process to make numerous berries of slightly

different sizes. Place into a plastic bag to stop them drying out before dusting.

Colouring

3 Dust each of the berries to various depths; starting with the smaller berries, dust with a mixture of moss and primrose and a tinge of red petal dust. As the berries mature, increase the amount of red and also add some aubergine. Allow to dry. Dip each berry into a full glaze, shake off excess and allow to dry. Tape over each of the stems with ¼-width nile green floristry tape.

Calyx

4 Roll out a small piece of green flower paste, leaving a bump at the centre. Cut out a calyx shape using either of the two sizes of stephanotis cutter (this will depend upon the size of the berry). Imagine the shape as a figure and, using a celstick, broaden the head and legs, using a rolling action. Place the shape on to a pad and soften all of the sepals.

5 Dust the edges of the calyx with the primrose and moss green mixture. Moisten the centre of the calyx with egg white and thread on to the back of the berry. Pull all of the sepals back. Allow to dry.

Leaves

6 Roll out some green flower paste, leaving a thick ridge down the centre. Place either the template or fresh hypericum leaf on top of the paste and cut out the shape using a sharp scalpel. Insert a moistened 28-gauge or 26-gauge wire, depending on the size of the leaf, into the thick ridge. You will need to insert the wire into at least half the length of the leaf.

7 Place the leaf on to the back of the fresh hypericum leaf and press the two together using the flat part of your hand. Place the leaf on to a pad and soften the edges. Reinforce the central vein by pinching the leaf on the back from the tip to the base. Allow to firm up before dusting.

8 Dust with moss and dark green petal dust, making the back very pale. Dust a little aubergine petal dust on to the edges and at the base of each leaf. Dip into a ½ glaze, shake off the excess and allow to dry. Using a sharp scalpel, etch some fine veins on to the leaf.

Assembly

9 Tape the berries together into groups of two and three. Join two groups together and add two leaves at the axil. Repeat this process several times to form lots of groups. Start a main stem with one of the groups taped on to an 18-gauge wire using ½-width nile green floristry tape. Tape some pairs of leaves at intervals down this stem. Repeat and make another stem. Join these two together, taping two leaves at the axil again. Continue this method until you have completed the required length. Dust the stems with aubergine, red and moss green petal dust. Bend each of the stems into shape using pliers.

AMARYLLIS

Originally botanists grouped this flower (*Hippeastrum*) with the true amaryllis (*Amaryllis belladonna*): unfortunately the name has stuck. Amaryllis originate from tropical and subtropical rainforests of South America and the Caribbean. They are often given as gifts at Christmastime as pot plants and it is in this form that most people associate them. However, they are also used as cut flowers and in bridal bouquets during the winter season. The variety pictured here is one of the smaller types of amaryllis, making it more suitable for wedding cakes.

MATERIALS

White, poppy and pale green flower paste
18, 24 and 26-gauge wires
Lemon, red, aubergine, dark green, vine and moss green petal dust (blossom tint)
Scarlet craft dust

EQUIPMENT

Fine-nosed pliers
White and nile green floristry tape
Amaryllis petal templates (see page 156)
Small narrow and side of petal amaryllis veiners (GI)
Large wide amaryllis veiner (GI)
Sharp scalpel

STAMENS

1 Cut two lengths of 26-gauge wire into thirds. Using a pair of fine-nosed pliers, bend a flat hook at one end of the wire, then hold the hook halfway down its length with pliers and bend it again to form a 'T' bar shape. Thicken the length of each stamen with a few layers of ¼-width white floristry tape, making them finer towards the anther. Repeat to make six stamens.

2 Attach a small sausage of white flower paste over the 'T' bars to form anthers. You will not need to use egg white for this. The size of the anther depends on how mature the flower is – a mature flower would have smaller anthers. Using a scalpel, indent a line on to the upper surface of the anther. Dust the anthers with lemon petal dust. Dust the length of the stamen with either red petal dust or scarlet craft dust (the latter gives a much richer red colour).

PISTIL

3 Roll a ball of poppy-coloured flower paste and insert a 24-gauge wire. Work the paste firmly and quickly between your finger and thumb to cover a good length of the wire. The pistil should not be longer than any of the petals. Smooth the pistil between the palms of your hands and trim off the excess paste. Using a small pair of scissors, cut the end of the pistil into three sections. Round off the sides of each of the sections, then curl them back a little. Bend the whole length of the pistil into a very lazy 'S' shape (see photograph). Dust the pistil with red or scarlet craft dust, leaving the end much paler to allow the base colour to show through. Allow to dry.

4 Tape the six stamens on to the pistil using ½-width green floristry tape, making the pistil a little longer. Using pliers, bend each of the stamens to follow the shape of the pistil.

Petals

5 I find that when I am making red flowers, it is better to start off a lot paler than I want the finished flower to be. If the paste is coloured deep red to begin with, then the end result is too dense and artificial. Roll out some mid-poppy coloured (or whatever your chosen colour is) flower paste, leaving a thick ridge down the centre (use a grooved board if you wish). Using a scalpel and the amaryllis templates made from the outlines on page 156, cut out the left, right and central petals.

6 Insert a moistened 26-gauge wire into the thick ridge of each, making sure that the wire supports at least half the length of the petals. Vein the left and right petals using the medium curved veiner from the small amaryllis set. Remove from the veiner, place on a pad and soften the edges gently using the rounded end of a large celstick (do not frill them).

7 Pinch each petal at the tips and at the base, and occasionally curl the edges at the base in slightly (this adds some interest and gives variation). Allow the petals to firm a little before dusting.

8 Vein the central petal using the narrow veiner in the set. Soften and dry as before.

9 Repeat the process for the larger outer sepals. You might need to use a 24-gauge wire for these sepals. Vein using the large amaryllis veiner from the larger set. Soften the edges of the sepals and then draw down a central vein using the dresden tool. Pinch the base and the tips of the sepals. Dry as before.

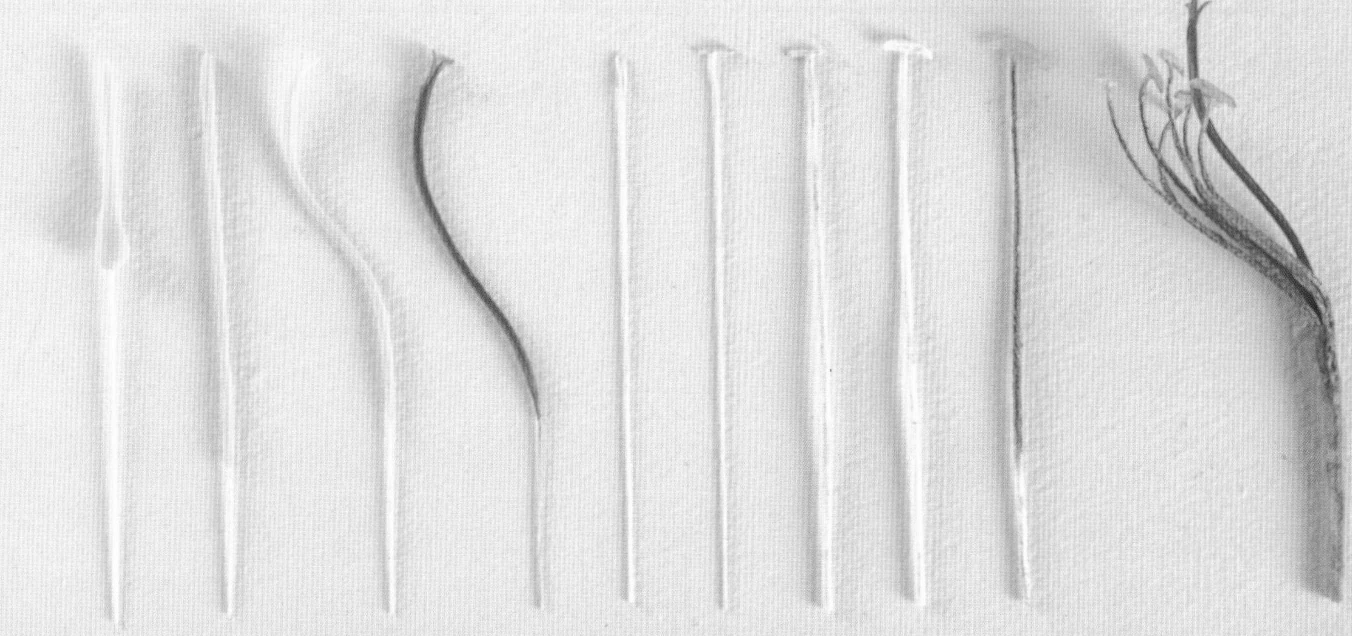

Colouring and Assembly

10 Dust each of the petals and sepals using either red petal dust or with scarlet craft dust (as shown). Start by dusting the edges of the petals/sepals and then gradually bring the colour down to cover the majority of the paste. Dust the base of each of the petals/sepals with aubergine and catch the edges with a tiny amount of aubergine, just to break up the red a little. When you have done this, there should be a little aubergine left on the brush. Use this to dust across the veins on each petal to highlight them.

11 Tape the left and right petals on to the stamens, so that the stamens curl towards them. Add the narrow petal underneath the stamens. Position the large sepals behind and in between each of the petals and tape the flower together tightly using ½-width nile green floristry tape. As the paste is still soft, you should be able to adjust the petals to give a more natural, relaxed finish. Tape an 18-gauge wire alongside the existing stem to strengthen the flower.

Buds

12 Tape over a half length of 18-gauge wire with green floristry tape. Bend a large hook on the end. Roll a large ball of poppy coloured flower paste into a teardrop shape, moisten the hooked wire and insert it into the fine end of the teardrop. Allow to dry.

13 Roll out and cut out three sepals as for the flower, but this time do not wire them. Vein and soften as before. Moisten the teardrop and attach the sepals to the cone. Pinch from the tips of the sepals down to the base, so that you form a ridge on each of the sepals. Dust as for the flower.

Assembly

14 Thicken the flower and bud stems with strips of absorbent kitchen paper and tape over with full-width floristry tape. Group the flowers and buds into groups of a maximum of five. Dust the stems with dark green, vine and moss green petal dust.

Note

Amaryllis come in a range of different shades and combinations of red, pink, peach, burgundy, green and white. Some varieties have very strong, striped designs on their petals. For most of the other coloured flowers, use cream or white flower paste, then dust to the required finish.

RUSCUS

Ruscus has very curious flattened stems that look like leaves called cladodes. It is from the centre, often on the back of each of the cladodes, that the plant produces its insignificant flowers and more substantial red fruit. Sometimes the fruit is still in place when you buy the foliage from a florist shop. There are several varieties of ruscus, some with more oval shaped leaves and others like the one shown here with very pointed leaves. It is only the plant's 'leaves' that are used in floristry, and these are simple to make in sugar. To make things easier they will be referred to as leaves in the text.

MATERIALS

Mid-green flower paste
Dark green petal dust (blossom tint)
20 and 28-gauge wires
¾ glaze (see page 151)

EQUIPMENT

Ruscus cutters (CC)
Fresh or dried ruscus
Sharp scalpel
Nile green floristry tape

LEAVES

1 Roll out a small piece of mid-green flower paste thinly, leaving a thicker central ridge. Cut out the leaf (cladode) using either the ruscus cutters or by using a fresh piece of ruscus as a template. Insert a moistened 28-gauge wire into the thick ridge, so that it supports at least half the length of the leaf.

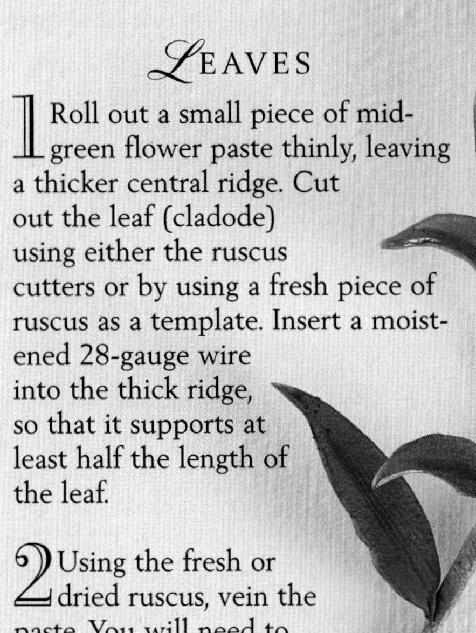

2 Using the fresh or dried ruscus, vein the paste. You will need to apply pressure on to the paste as the veining is very subtle. Pinch the leaf from the tip to the base on the back. Repeat the process to make numerous leaves in various sizes.

3 Dust heavily with dark green petal dust on the upper surface and a little on the back. When the leaves are dry, dip them into a ¾ glaze. Shake off the excess and allow to dry. Tape the leaves together into groups of two and three. Then tape them on to a 20-gauge wire, starting with one set of leaves and then spiral further groups down the main stem. Dust the main stems with the dark green mixture.

SUMMER GARDEN WEDDING

This spectacular wedding cake was designed and decorated by Tony Warren and displayed on the Table of Honour at the International British Sugarcraft Guild Exhibition 1997. I have rearranged the floral display to include cosmos and other flowers. It would form a magnificent centrepiece for a reception held in a garden marquee.

MATERIALS

20cm (8 in) and 30cm (12 in) teardrop-shaped cakes
Apricot glaze
2kg (4lb) almond paste (marzipan)
Clear alcohol (kirsch or vodka)
3kg (6lb) champagne sugarpaste
Pink royal icing
Apricot, fuchsia, white and pearl white petal dust (blossom tint)
Fine colonial rose ribbon to trim cakes
Picot edge ivory and green braid ribbon to trim boards

EQUIPMENT

Sugarpaste smoothers
28cm (11 in) and 38cm (15 in) teardrop-shaped cake boards
Broad flat paintbrush
No. 1 piping tube (tip)
Home-made tilting stand and 45cm (18 in) thin oval base
Sage green material
Pot of velverette fabric glue
Double-sided carpet tape
Perspex separator
Florists' staysoft
Florists' binding tape

FLOWERS

3 oriental hybrid lilies and 1 bud (see page 91)
5 pink cosmos (see page 86)
2 stems of agapanthus (see page 98)
5 stems of sweet peas (see page 46)
7 roses (see page 136)
4 stems of Solomon's seal (see page 100)
3 stems of bells of Ireland (see page 89)
10 stems of ivy (see page 114)

PREPARATION

1 Brush the surface of the cakes with apricot glaze and cover with almond paste. Allow to dry overnight. Moisten the surface of the almond paste with clear alcohol and cover with champagne sugarpaste, using smoothers to obtain a good finish. Cover the cake boards with champagne sugarpaste. Transfer the cakes to the boards, making sure that you have a very neat join between the base of the cakes and the boards. Allow to dry.

2 Mix together apricot, fuchsia and white petal dust, and then dilute with clear alcohol. Using a broad, flat paintbrush, paint uneven strokes of colour on to the sides of the cake and on the board. Allow to dry, then dust over with pearl white petal dust (optional).

3 Attach a band of fine rose ribbon around the base of both of the cakes, then pipe a snail trail over the top using royal icing and a piping bag fitted with a no. 1 piping tube. Glue the picot edge ivory ribbon to the edge of the boards using a non-toxic glue stick.

ASSEMBLY

4 Adhere the sage green material on to the thin oval board using the velverette fabric glue. Stretch the material to make a smooth neat surface and glue the excess neatly to the underside of the board. Attach the band of green braid to the board edge. Place the bottom tier of the cake on to this board. Position the top tier on to the tilting part of the stand, held in place with double-sided carpet tape.

5 Place the perspex separator upside down behind the base tier. Attach a clump of staysoft and hold in place using florists' binding tape. Attractively arrange the flowers and foliage in a free-style unstructured manner into the staysoft to complete the design.

COSMOS

Cultivated in Europe since the eighteenth century, the cosmos (*Cosmea sulphureaus*) is a bright, showy and very popular summer garden flower. It comes in a range of different colours which include pink, red, white, lavender, orange and yellow. (There is also another species that has dark brown burgundy flowers with a scent of chocolate. However this is much smaller and has a different type of foliage – see page 88.) The size of cosmos flowers varies – the one that I have made is a slightly smaller species. There are also double forms of cosmos flowers. This is one of the easiest and most effective flowers I have ever made.

MATERIALS

White seed-head stamens
20, 24, 28 and 30-gauge white wires
Cyclamen liquid food colouring
Lemon, plum, aubergine, moss and dark green petal dust (blossom tint)
Deep magenta craft dust
Pale ruby, white, pale and mid-green flower paste

EQUIPMENT

Nile green floristry tape
Small stencil brush
Australian rose petal cutters (TT349-352)
Small cosmos veiner (GI)
Pointed daisy cutter (TT106)

STAMENS

1 Take ¼ - ⅓ of a bunch of seed-head stamens and bend them in half to double the amount. Try to keep the tips at roughly the same height. Tape them on to a 24-gauge wire, making sure that they are not too long. Trim away any excess stamen from the base and tape down to the end of the wire. Using cyclamen liquid colouring and a stiff stencil brush, colour the stamens. While the tips are still damp, dip them into some lemon petal dust to form the pollen. Shake off any excess and allow the stamens to dry thoroughly.

PETALS

2 First of all bend each of the Australian rose petal cutters to make them a more narrow shape, by simply pressing the sides together with your fingers and thumb. Roll out some ruby coloured flower paste, not too thinly on to a grooved board. Cut out eight petals using

your chosen size of cutter (I tend to use a mixture of sizes in an arrangement). Cut several lengths of 28-gauge wire into thirds, moisten the end of the wire and insert it into at least half the length of each petal. Pinch the base of each petal to secure it and form a slightly pointed shape. To make a larger flower, stretch the petal at this stage.

3 Vein each of the petals using the double-sided cosmos petal veiner. Remove from the veiner and place back on the board. Using the broad end of the dresden tool, work the edges to pull out three subtle points. Place the petal on to a pad and soften the sides using a celstick. Pinch each petal into shape and allow to firm with a slight curve at the end.

COLOURING AND ASSEMBLY

4 The colouring depends on your personal taste; some of the flowers have only a patch of colour at the base and others are very bright and bold. My preference is to use deep magenta craft dust or plum petal dust to colour the main part of the petal, and then to dust a patch of aubergine at the base. In an arrangement where the cosmos is the main flower, use a mixture of various pinks and white.

5 Tape the petals around the stamens using ½-width nile green floristry tape. Add a 20-gauge wire to lengthen and strengthen the stem. As the petals should be still wet at this stage, you can now re-shape them or squash them together to form a partially open flower. Allow to dry, then steam to remove the dusty effect.

CALYX

6 The cosmos has a double calyx. The first layer is made by forming a ball of pale green flower paste into a mexican hat shape. Place the shape, flat side down, on to a board. Roll out the paste using a celstick and then cut out the calyx shape with the daisy cutter. Before you remove the paste from the cutter, rub your thumb over the paste against the cutter to give a clean, neat cut to the calyx.

7 Re-roll the sepals using a celstick, then hollow the centre out using the pointed end of the tool. Place the calyx on to a pad and draw down a central vein on the inside of each of the sepals using the fine end of the dresden tool. Moisten the centre of the calyx with egg white and thread on to the back of the flower, removing any excess paste from the base.

8 To form the second layer of the calyx, roll eight very fine strands of mid-green flower paste; these should be pointed at one end. Using the flat side of a veiner, flatten each of the sepals. Attach them to the first calyx using egg white, positioning each of them in between each of

the sepals on the previous layer. Curl the tips back slightly. This method makes a very pretty but extremely fragile calyx. A simpler and safer method is to use floristry tape. Cut the tape into ¼ width and twist it back on itself to form a fine strand. Cut eight pieces and then tape on to the first layer using ½-width tape. Dust with a mixture of dark and moss green petal dust.

BUDS

9 Form a ball of pale green paste and insert a hooked, moistened 24-gauge wire into the base. Divide the surface of the ball into eight sections using a sharp scalpel. Flatten each alternate section using the broad end of the dresden tool. Dust with moss green and aubergine petal dust. Add the outer calyx as described for the flower.

LEAVES

10 In the past I have made these leaves in sugar, however they are very fragile and look a little too thick compared with those of the fresh flower. I now use floristry tape to achieve a more realistic and robust leaf. Using ½-width nile green tape, start by taping the end of a piece of 30-gauge wire. When you reach the end of the wire, continue to twist the tape back on itself to form a fine strand. Add another four pieces of twisted tape (no wire) to this main wire to form one leaf section. Repeat this to make another two leaf sections. Tape the three sections together to form one set of leaves. Dust with dark green and moss green petal dust.

ASSEMBLY

11 Tape together the buds and flowers of various sizes, adding a set of leaves every time you join them together. Continue to add sets of leaves to cover the length of the stem you require. Dust the main stem with a mixture of moss and dark green petal dust, and add a touch of plum and aubergine petal dust here and there.

NOTE

CHOCOLATE COSMOS

I mentioned that this flower smells of chocolate – it actually smells more like drinking chocolate to me!

To make the flower, use one of the smaller Australian rose petal cutters and pale brown flower paste. Cut out eight petals, vein and work as described for the cosmos pictured. The petals should be cupped rather than being dried flat.

The stamens are made in the same way as the flower described, this time using a smaller group of stamens and omitting the addition of pollen to the tips.

Dust the petals in layers of aubergine, brown and nutkin brown petal dust – predominantly aubergine. Assemble the flower as before and add the calyx.

The leaves do not have a fern-like structure like the ones pictured, but are tri-lobed in shape and a greyish green in colour.

Bells of Ireland

This unusual plant (*Moluccella laevis*) derives its name from the large green bell-like calyces. The flower is very small in comparison to the calyx and is the shape of a nettle flower. Bells of Ireland used to be eaten as a vegetable and has been cultivated in Europe since the sixteenth century. Florists use the plant in both its fresh and dried state to add height and interest to arrangements and bouquets.

MATERIALS

White, pale holly/ivy and mid-green flower paste
18, 24, 26, 28 and 30-gauge wires
Vine green, holly/ivy, dark green, moss green and aubergine petal dust (blossom tint)
½ glaze (see page 151)

EQUIPMENT

Small set of rose petal cutters (TT)
1 fresh stem of bells of Ireland with leaves
Nile green or white floristry tape

Calyx

1 It is unusual to start with the calyx instead of the flower, but it is the calyx that provides the decoration in this instance. Bend a small hook on the end of either a 26-gauge or 24-gauge wire (this will depend upon the size of the calyx). Moisten the hook and attach a small cone of white paste. Mark the surface in half using a scalpel. You will need to make one of these buds for each calyx. Dry.

2 Roll a ball of pale green flower paste into a cone shape, then pinch the base out to form a mexican hat shape. Place the hat down on to the board and thin out the base using a celstick. Cut out the calyx shape using a rose petal cutter, making sure that the majority of the paste is at the pointed end of the rose petal shape.

3 Hollow out the base and the centre of the calyx using the pointed end of a large celstick to form the characteristic bell shape. (It would be a good idea to buy a fresh stem to form the correct shape.) Continue to press the sides of the calyx, using your thumb against the celstick, until you have made the edges of the calyx quite fine.

4 Pinch a few points around the edges of the calyx, using your

finger and thumb. Moisten the base of the bud and thread through the centre of the calyx. Curl back the edges if required to form a more attractive shape. You will need to make lots of calyces to complete a stem of bells of Ireland. The fresh stem has rings of six to eight calyces in graduating sizes from the tip to the base.

5 Dust the calyces to various degrees using vine, holly/ivy and a touch of dark green (the outer surface of each of the calyces should be much paler). Allow them to dry overnight.

6 Using a sharp scalpel, etch some fine veins on the inside of each of the calyces. This is optional as it can be very time-consuming – it does however look very good when completed.

FLOWERS

7 The flowers are not essential, but do add a little interest even if you only include a few on a whole stem! I have often bought this plant from the florist where it has either not come into flower yet or it is past its best and the flowers have dropped off. A flower-arranger recently told me that the flowers are often removed to enhance the appearance and to make them last a bit longer.

8 Form a ball of white flower paste into a teardrop shape. Using a fine pair of scissors, cut the teardrop in half to form two petals. Flatten each petal between your finger and thumb. Next divide the base of one of the petals into two and then trim the sides to form the petal shape. Frill and thin out the edges using the broad end of the dresden tool. Pinch a ridge down the centre using tweezers.

9 Hollow out the top to form a hood petal using a small celstick. Position inside a calyx using a small amount of egg white. Sometimes the flowers have a pink tinge to them.

LEAVES

10 Roll out some mid-green paste, leaving the centre slightly thicker. Using a fresh leaf as a template, cut out the leaf shape with a scalpel. Insert a 30-gauge or 28-gauge wire into the thick ridge. Use the fresh leaf to vein the paste. Pinch the central vein and allow to dry. You will need to make various sizes to complete a stem. The fresh bells of Ireland has a group of leaves at the top of the stem and is then followed by the rings of calyces, which have two leaves attached, one at either side at the base of each of the rings. As with the flowers, sometimes the florist and flower-arranger removes the leaves – this is an option that the sugarcrafter can happily pick up on.

11 Dust with holly/ivy and dark green petal dust. Glaze using a ½ glaze, shake off excess and leave to dry.

ASSEMBLY

12 If you are using leaves, start the stem with two tiny leaves. Tape in a few more pairs of leaves in graduating sizes using ½-width white or nile green floristry tape. Next, tape in a ring of small calyces and a pair of leaves (if using). Leave a gap on the stem and then add a slightly larger ring of calyces (and leaves.) As you tape down the stem you might need to add another couple of 18-gauge wires and some shredded absorbent kitchen paper to thicken and strengthen the stem. When you have completed the length of stem required, dust with a pale mixture of greens similar to those used on the calyces. Catch the edge of the calyces here and there with a touch of aubergine petal dust. Steam the whole stem to remove the dusty appearance left by the colour. Bend the stem into the required shape; real stems often twist to follow the light.

ORIENTAL HYBRID LILY

The oriental hybrid lilies originate from crosses made from *L. auratum*, *L.speciosum* and *L. rubrum*. They have predominantly white or pink flowers, with spots or speckling. The lily pictured is based on a variety called *Le rêve* which has pale pink flowers and only a small amount of speckling on each petal. The oriental lilies are always a popular choice for bridal bouquets, mainly due to their showy, exotic appearance and heavy scent.

STAMENS

1 Use a third of a length of 26-gauge white wires for each stamen. You will need six of these. Using a pair of fine-nosed pliers, bend a flat hook at one end of the wire, then hold the hook halfway down its length with the pliers and bend it again to form a 'T'- bar shape. Thicken the length (filaments) of each stamen with a few layers of ¼-width white floristry tape making them finer towards the anther. Dust with a pale mixture of primrose, moss green and white petal dust.

2 Attach a sausage of white paste over the 'T' bar to form the anther. Mix together some mimosa sugartex with skintone and lemon petal dust to form a pollen mixture. Paint the anthers with a little egg white, then dip into the pollen mix. Allow to dry thoroughly.

PISTIL

3 Roll a ball of pale green flower paste and insert a moistened 24-gauge wire. Work the paste firmly between your finger and thumb in a rubbing motion and try to cover a

MATERIALS

18, 24 and 26-gauge white wires
Primrose, moss green, white, skintone, aubergine, deep purple, plum, fuchsia, pink, lemon and dark green petal dust (blossom tint)
White, pale and mid-green flower paste
Mimosa sugartex
Egg white
½ glaze
Cyclamen liquid food colouring

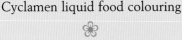

EQUIPMENT

Fine-nosed pliers
White and nile green floristry tape
Medium casablanca lily cutters (TT)
Casablanca lily veiners (GI)

good length of the wire. (The pistil should measure at least the length of one of the petals.) Smooth the pistil between the palms of your hands and then trim away any excess paste. Flatten the top of the pistil and then using a pair of tweezers, pinch the end into three sections. Flatten the top again if needed, then divide the upper surface into three using a sharp scalpel. Bend the whole pistil slightly to make it more natural looking. Attach another piece of green paste at the base to represent the ovary. Divide into six using a sharp scalpel.

4 Colour the pistil with a mixture of moss and primrose petal dust, making the ovary stronger in colour. The tip of the pistil is coloured with a touch of aubergine and deep purple. To make a mature pistil, add a drop of glaze to the tip.

5 Tape the stamens around the pistil, making the pistil higher than the stamens. Bend the stamens into the required position.

PETALS

6 Roll out some white flower paste, leaving a thick ridge down the centre. Using the wide petal cutter, cut out three petals. Insert a moistened 24-gauge wire into each

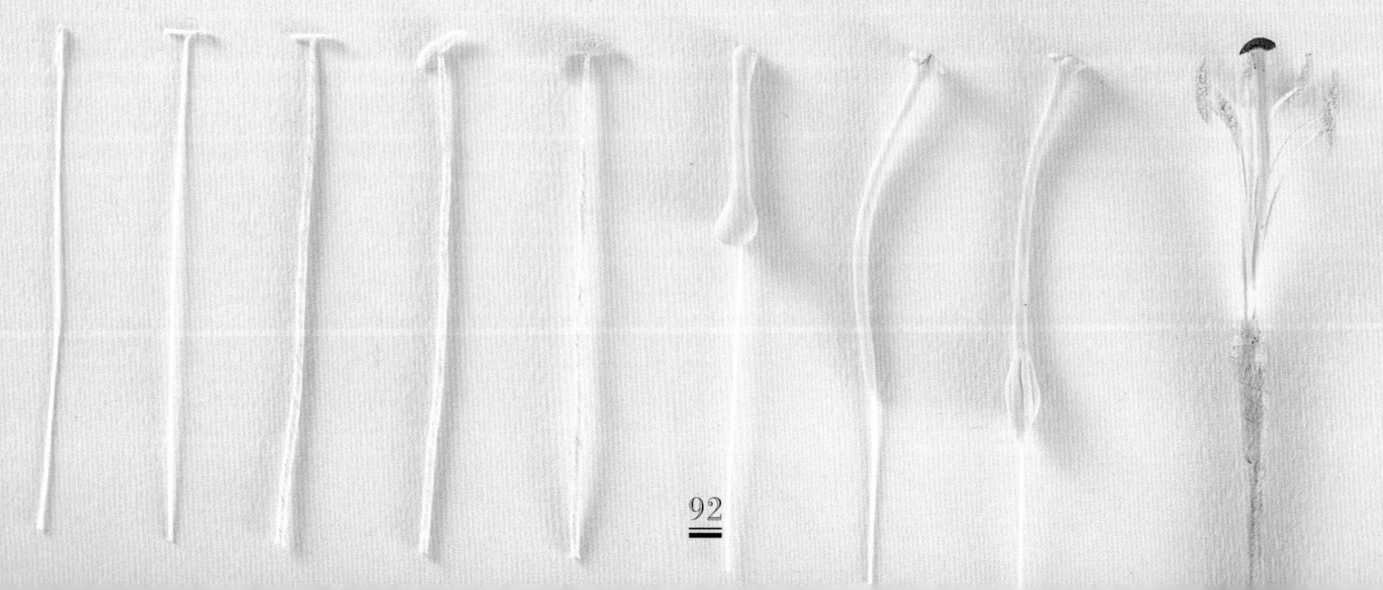

petal, taking the wire up into at least half the length of the petal.

7 Vein each of the petals using the large casablanca veiners, pressing the two sides together firmly to give a good impression. Place the petals on a pad and soften the edges using the rounded end of a celstick. Pinch down the centre of the each petal, especially at the tips. Repeat the process to cut out three narrow petals. Dry over a curve until firm enough to handle.

COLOURING

8 Dust the base of each petal with primrose, and then over-dust half of this area with moss green. The main depth of colouring of the flower depends on your personal taste as there are slight variations. Mix together plum, fuchsia or pink with white petal dust, and colour the petals using a flat brush. Keep the pink away from the primrose at the base otherwise you will end up with a slight orange tone. The narrow petals have less colour on them.

9 Using a fine paintbrush and a little cyclamen liquid colouring, paint on the specks of colour. (It is a good idea to have a fresh flower or good photograph to copy at this stage.)

10 Dust the tips of the petals with the brush you used for the primrose and moss green. The colour should be very pale; cleaning your brush with cornflour (cornstarch) will help to give a more subtle finish.

ASSEMBLY

11 Start by taping the larger petals around the base of the stamens using ½-width nile green floristry tape. Add the smaller petals in between each of the larger ones, slightly recessed. As the petals should be still slightly soft at this stage, you can now re-curl them if needed. Dust the back of the flower with the moss and primrose mixture, making it darker at the base. Tape each flower on to an 18-gauge wire for strength.

BUDS

12 Tape over an 18-gauge wire with ½-width nile green floristry tape. Bend a large open hook in one end and moisten with egg white. Roll a large sausage of paste and insert the wire into one end, making sure that it is firmly fixed.

13 To mark an impression of the petals, make a 'cage' using three 24-gauge wires taped at the base. Open the cage and insert the bud, tip first. Arrange the wires equally and close them together so that they press into the paste and mark it equally into three sections. Release the cage and move each of the wires a few millimetres to one side. Close the cage again to form three ridges down the length of the bud. Remove the cage and then, using your finger and thumb, pinch a deep ridge on the paste between each pair of division lines.

14 Dust the bud with a small amount of the flower colour, and then over-dust with the primrose and moss green mixture. The base of the bud should be slightly darker so increase the moss green at the base. The smaller the buds are, the more green they should be.

15 Steam both the flowers and buds to give a waxy appearance and to seal the colour on to the petals (see page 151).

LEAVES

16 Roll out some mid-green paste, leaving a thick ridge down the centre. Cut out the leaves using a sharp scalpel. Insert a moistened 24 or 26-gauge wire depending on the size of the leaf into at least half the length of the ridge on each leaf. Place each on a pad and soften the edges using the largest celstick. Vein either by marking with the fine end of the dresden tool or with a double-sided veiner, or with the fresh leaf. Allow to dry until firm enough to handle.

17 Dust the leaves with dark green and moss green petal dust. The smaller leaves should be more of a lime green in colour. Dip each leaf into a ½ glaze, shake off excess and leave to dry.

HEARTS ENTWINED

This dramatic creation offers an unusual alternative for a single-tiered wedding cake design. The idea is that it represents two hearts – one with the heart-shaped cake and the other with curved stems of the flowers and foliage.

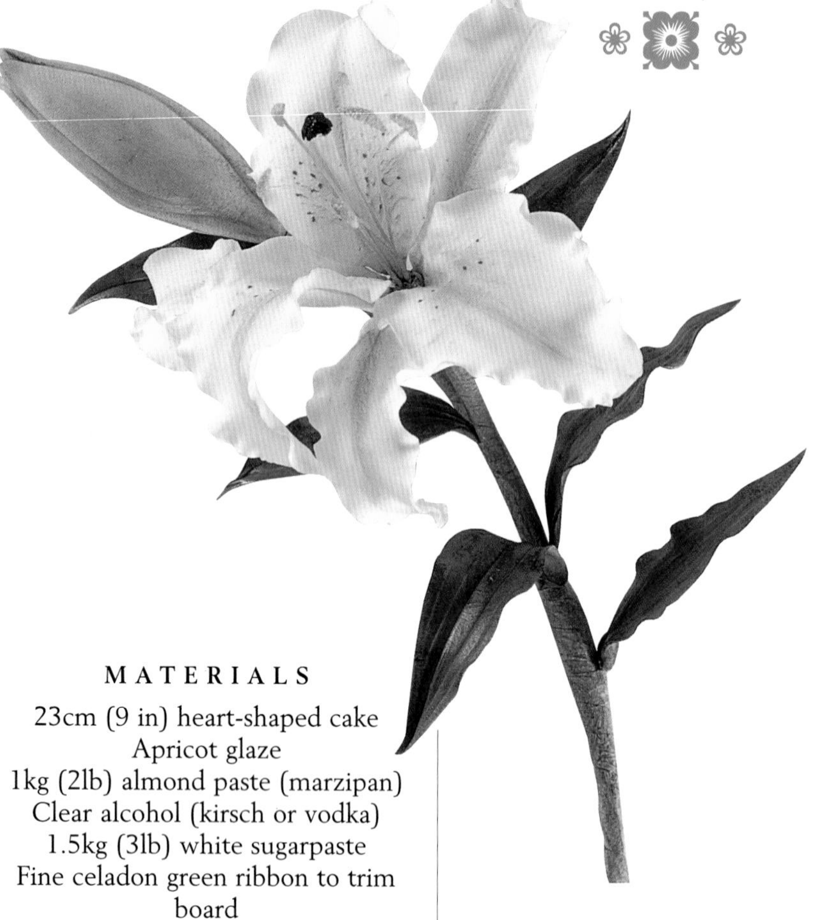

MATERIALS

23cm (9 in) heart-shaped cake
Apricot glaze
1kg (2lb) almond paste (marzipan)
Clear alcohol (kirsch or vodka)
1.5kg (3lb) white sugarpaste
Fine celadon green ribbon to trim board
175g (6oz) green sugarpaste

EQUIPMENT

23cm (9 in) heart-shaped cake board
23cm (9 in) heart-shaped thin cake board (optional)
Rectangular bonsai dish

FLOWERS

Hearts Entwined Arrangement (see page 97)
2 stems of Solomon's seal (see page 100)
A few extra pieces of ivy (see page 114)

PREPARATION

1 Place the heart cake on to the reverse side of the 23cm (9 in) cake board and adhere with a little softened sugarpaste. Brush the cake with apricot glaze and cover with almond paste. Leave to dry for 1 week. Brush the surface of the almond paste with clear alcohol and cover the cake with white sugarpaste, using sugarpaste smoothers and the sugarpaste pad method to achieve a good smooth finish (see Note). Allow to dry.

2 You now need to decide whether or not you want to cover the silver cake board at the back or not. You can leave the back of the cake with the silver board showing; trim the board edge with fine green ribbon, if liked. Alternatively, cover the 23cm (9 in) heart-shaped thin board with white sugarpaste. Crimp the edge if preferred. Allow to dry. Attach some double-sided tape on to the back of the thin board and stick it to the silver side of the cake board on the back of the cake.

ASSEMBLY

3 Roll out some green sugarpaste and line the rectangular bonsai dish. Position, embed and secure the cake on its side into the green paste.

4 Place the Hearts Entwined Arrangement in front of the cake and curve the stems more if required to follow the shape of the cake. Insert two stems of Solomon's seal in the sugarpaste behind the cake, arching their stems over the cake to complete the design. Add a few extra pieces of ivy at the base.

NOTE

As well as using smoothers, a good way to achieve a silky smooth finish on sugarpaste is to flatten a ball of sugarpaste in the palm of your hand and to smooth it over the paste. This is especially good for smoothing the top edges of cakes.

HEARTS ENTWINED ARRANGEMENT

This beautifully elegant arrangement can be taken directly from the Hearts Entwined wedding cake after the reception and used as a room decoration as a reminder of the wedding day.

FLOWERS

2 stems of Solomon's seal (see page 100)
1 oriental hybrid lily (see page 91)
2 stems of agapanthus (see page 98)
Several pieces of ivy (see page 114)
3 pink half roses and 2 pink rosebuds (see page 136)
11 stems of lily-of-the-valley (see page 54)
Extra leaves/foliage

EQUIPMENT

Florists' staysoft
Green oval bonsai dish
Glue gun and glue sticks
18-gauge wire
Nile green floristry tape
Pliers
Wire cutters

PREPARATION

1 Position a ball of florists' staysoft offset on to the bonsai dish, using a small amount of glue from the glue gun. Strengthen any of the longer flower stems, using 18-gauge wire alongside the main stems.

ASSEMBLY

2 First of all, hook the end of the tallest stem of Solomon's seal (this will help it stand in such a small amount of staysoft). Insert it into the staysoft, arching its stem over to form an attractive outline. Next insert the small stem of Solomon's seal to form a basic 'L' shape.

3 Trim the length of the lily stem, hook the end and position it centrally into the staysoft to form the focal point.

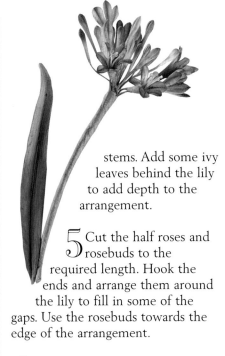

4 Hook the ends of the agapanthus stems and insert them, one next to each of the Solomon's seal stems. Add some ivy leaves behind the lily to add depth to the arrangement.

5 Cut the half roses and rosebuds to the required length. Hook the ends and arrange them around the lily to fill in some of the gaps. Use the rosebuds towards the edge of the arrangement.

6 Finally insert the lily-of-the-valley in groups into the staysoft at three separate points of the arrangement. Add any extra foliage to fill in any gaps in the design.

AGAPANTHUS

If I am asked to include a blue flower on a wedding cake, this is the flower that immediately springs to my mind! Its name translated from the Greek means the flower of love (*agape* – love, *panthus* – flower) so it is an appropriate choice as a bridal flower. Orginating from South Africa but mainly cultivated in Holland, agapanthus is not a difficult flower to make. It covers a large range of different shades of blue, but for those who do not like blue there is also a white form.

STAMENS

1 Tape six stamens on to a 24-gauge wire using ¼-width nile green floristry tape. Add an extra stamen to represent the pistil (in the fresh flower this is shorter than the stamens – I tend to make it longer as it makes the flower look prettier). Dust the tips of the stamens first with primrose, then over-dust with a touch of deep purple. Curl the stamens slightly.

FLOWER

2 Roll a ball of white or pale cream flower paste into a cone shape. Pinch the broad end of the cone between your fingers and thumb to thin out the base and form a pedestal shape. Place the flat part of the pedestal against the board and roll out using a celstick. Try to form a neat waistline around the thick area of the pedestal.

3 Cut out the flower using the agapanthus cutter. Before you remove the paste from the cutter, rub your thumb over the paste against the cutter to make sure the petals have cleanly cut edges.

4 Place the flower flat side down on a board. The agapanthus has three petals broader than the other three – this is reflected in the cutter shape. However you will still need to broaden each of the six petals slightly using a celstick and a rolling motion.

5 Open up the centre of the flower using the pointed end of the celstick. Press the base of each petal against the stick to form a graceful shape to the back of the flower.

6 Place the flower on to a pad and, using the fine end of the dresden tool, draw down a vein on the back of each petal. Turn the flower over and draw a vein on the front in exactly the same position as the veins on the back. Pinch the tips of each flower slightly.

7 Moisten the base of the stamens and pull them down into the centre of the flower. Neaten the back of the flower and remove any excess paste. Arrange the petals so that the broader ones are slightly

MATERIALS

White seed-head stamens
18, 24 and 28-gauge wires
Primrose, deep purple, lavender, white, bluebell, moss and vine green petal dust (blossom tint)
White or pale cream flower paste
Clear alcohol (kirsch or vodka)

EQUIPMENT

Nile green floristry tape
Agapanthus cutter (TT516)

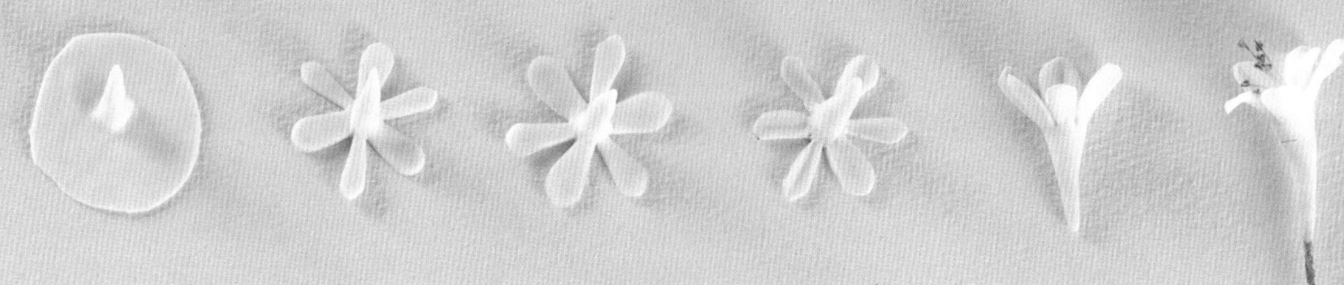

higher in position. Curve the whole flower so that the stamens are closer to one side.

COLOURING

8 Dust the flower with a mixture of lavender, white and bluebell, starting at the edges and dusting towards the centre of the flower (keep the centre white). Over-dust the edges with deep purple. Dust the centre and the back of the flower with a small amount of primrose and moss green petal dust.

9 Each of the petals has a darker line running down the centre. Dilute some deep purple petal dust with a small amount of clear alcohol. Paint a strong vein down the centre of each of the petals.

BUDS

10 Hook and moisten the end of a 24-gauge wire. Roll a ball of paste into a cone shape and insert the hooked wire into the fine end. Neaten the base of the cone again. Form the broad end of the cone into a slight point to form the tip. Using a cage with three 28-gauge wires, insert the bud tip first. Mark the petals and then move each of the wires slightly to one side and mark again to form three narrow ridges. Pinch the broad sections slightly, between your finger and thumb. You will need to make many buds of various sizes to form a complete umbel. Dust the buds with the same combination as the flowers, using more green on the smaller buds.

ASSEMBLY

11 Agapanthus flowers are often used as individual pipped flowers in sprays and corsages, but if you want to create more impact in an arrangement or bouquet, use them as a complete umbel. Tape the buds on to an 18-gauge wire using ½-width floristry tape (the smaller buds will have shorter stems). Next add the flowers (you will need between five and seven flowers at least). Thicken the stem with a couple more 18-gauge wires and also tape in some shredded absorbent kitchen paper to form more bulk. Dust the stem with a mixture of moss and vine green.

12 The leaves are very long and straplike, and are not used generally in floral arrangements.

NOTE

Agapanthus is available for many months of the year, with a peak during the summer. There can be as many as 200 flowers on one umbel of agapanthus. Fortunately this is not required by the sugarcrafter!

SOLOMON'S SEAL

It is not known for certain why Solomon's seal (*Polygonatum*) has its rather grand name. One theory is that it was because of the medicinal value of the plant for 'sealing' wounds and healing broken bones, and also as a cure for black eyes. It is traditionally said that the biblical King Solomon approved of its use! The flower shown here has been based on a garden variety. They can also be obtained as a cut flower from the florist. Solomon's seal can either be used as long trailing stems or they can be pipped and used individually in sprays and bouquets.

MATERIALS

Fine white stamens
18, 24, 26, 30 and 33-gauge wires
Primrose, moss, holly/ivy and dark green petal dust (blossom tint)
White and mid-green flower paste
¼ glaze (see page 151)

EQUIPMENT

Nile green floristry tape
Six petal pointed blossom cutters (N6,N7)
Solomon's seal leaf veiners (GI)

STAMENS

1 Tape six fine stamens on to the end of a short length of 30-gauge wire using ¼-width nile green floristry tape. Dust the tips with a touch of primrose petal dust. Place to one side and wash your hands because you need the flowers to be white not pale yellow!

FLOWER

2 Form a ball of well kneaded white flower paste into a teardrop shape. Pinch out the broad end of the teardrop to form a pedestal shape. Place the pedestal, with the flat side down, on to a board. Thin out the paste using a small celstick.

3 Cut out the flower shape using either of the two sizes of six petal blossom cutters – you will need a mixture of sizes to complete a stem. The backs of the flowers are

quite heavy and, because of this, you would be advised to place the back of the pedestal into a hole on the firm side of a celpad. Place the cutter over the flat section of paste and cut out the flower. Remove the cut out flower from the hole.

4 Soften the edges of each of the petals to thin them out a little. Open up the throat of the flower using the pointed end of a small celstick. Press the sides of the flower against the stick to thin them out and to give the flower more of a bell shape. The flower should be bulbous at the base, then have a waistline and then the petals should flair out a little at the base.

5 Place the flower, face side up, against your finger. Draw down a central vein on each petal using the fine end of the dresden tool. Pinch the tips of each of the petals and then arrange them so that it looks as if three of the alternate petals are on the inside layer and three on the outside. Curl their tips back a little. You will need to make a lot of flowers as they are grouped in twos and threes down the stem.

6 Dust the tips of the petals and the base of each flower with a mixture of primrose and moss green.

BUDS

7 Tape over several short lengths of 33-gauge wire with ¼-width nile green floristry tape. Bend a small hook in the end of each one. Roll a small ball of white flower paste into a cone shape and insert the hooked wire into the base. Roll the cone shape so that it resembles the shape of the flower but it needs to have a slight point at the tip too. Dust the tips and the base of each bud as for the flower.

LEAVES

8 Roll out a piece of mid-green paste, leaving a thick ridge down the centre. Using one of the Solomon's seal leaf veiners, press the flat side on top of the paste to leave an imprint of the basic outline. Cut out the leaf shape using a scalpel.

9 Insert a moistened 26-gauge or 24-gauge wire, depending on the size of the leaf, into the thick ridge. Place in between the two sides of the leaf veiner and press firmly to achieve a defined impression. Place the leaf on a pad and soften the edges using the rounded end of a large celstick. Pinch the leaf at the back from the tip to the base to shape the leaf. Allow to firm up over a slight curve before dusting.

COLOURING AND ASSEMBLY

10 Dust the leaf in layers with moss, holly/ivy and some dark green petal dust. Dip into a ¼ glaze, shake off the excess and allow the leaf to dry.

11 Tape the buds and flowers into sets of two and three, using ¼-width nile green tape. To form a long arched stem, tape a smaller leaf on to the end of an 18-gauge wire using ½-width nile green tape. Add a couple more slightly larger leaves, alternating them on the stem. Start adding the groups of buds, which should dangle below the stem. Every time you add a set of buds or flowers, you need to tape in a leaf at the axil. As you work down the stem you might need to add more 18-gauge wire to give strength to the stem.

12 Dust the main and shorter stems with a mixture of the various greens used on the leaves. Bend the flowers down and the leaves up using pliers, then bend the whole stem into its characteristic arched shape.

CHEERFUL HARMONY

This two-tiered cake with its wonderful tangled mass of Iceland poppies would be most suited to a couple who would like their wedding just that little bit different. The design conjures up an immediate representation of hot summer days, mainly due to the glorious colour combination of orange, peach, red and yellow. This is the cake that I created for the Table of Honour at the International British Sugarcraft Guild Exhibition 1997.

MATERIALS

15cm (6 in) and 30cm (12 in) oval cakes
Apricot glaze
2kg (4lb) almond paste (marzipan)
Clear alcohol (kirsch or vodka)
3kg (6lb) champagne sugarpaste
Fine red ribbon to trim cakes
Royal icing
Broad burnt orange ribbon to trim boards
Tangerine, red, green and skintone petal dust (blossom tint)

EQUIPMENT

Sugarpaste smoothers
23cm (9 in) and 40cm (16 in) oval cake boards
Border stencil design (SL)
Firm soft medium paintbrush
Sharp scalpel
Fine paintbrush
Thin perspex disc
Small fleur-de-lys candle holder
Florists' staysoft
Two small perspex discs

FLOWERS

12 Iceland poppies, assorted colours (see page 107)
about 14 Iceland poppy buds

PREPARATION

1 Cover both cake boards with champagne sugarpaste and allow to dry. Using tangerine petal dust and a firm soft paintbrush, colour the area of the boards that will be exposed once the cakes are positioned. Use a stippling action with the brush to achieve a more interesting texture and to adhere a strong colour to the boards. Over-dust with red petal dust using the stippling action again (some of the tangerine base colour should show through). Dilute a little of the red petal dust with a small amount of clear alcohol (if you have too much alcohol the finished result will be patchy and very sticky). Place the stencil on top

of the dusted board and, using the stippling action again, apply the diluted red colour. (The stencil design I used was quite complicated so I picked out parts of the design to simplify and create an individual design.) Allow to dry. Using as sharp scalpel, etch around the edges of each of the stencilled shapes to highlight and define the design.

2 Brush the cakes with apricot glaze and cover with almond paste. Allow to dry overnight. Moisten the surface of the almond paste with clear alcohol and cover the cakes with champagne sugarpaste, using sugarpaste smoothers to achieve a good finish. Position the cakes on the cake boards and allow to dry for a few days.

3 Using the same stencil as before, add a design to the top of both cakes. This time use the orange and red petal dusts mixed with alcohol to create the design. Add extra hand-painted details using a finer paintbrush and orange, red and green dusts diluted with alcohol.

4 Fasten two bands of red ribbon around the base of each cake using a small amount of royal icing. Attach the broad burnt orange ribbon to the board edges using a non-toxic glue stick.

ASSEMBLY

5 Position the thin perspex disc on to the centre of the bottom tier and place the fleur-de-lys candle holder on top. Position the smaller cake on top, making sure that the complete display looks balanced.

6 Attach a clump of florists' staysoft on to each of the small perspex discs using a glue gun and place one at the back of each cake. Start to position the main focal flowers, inserting the end of each stem into the staysoft. You will soon reach the stage where you will have to dismantle the cakes before you can carry on and complete the arrangements. With this design it is important to tangle the flowers and buds as much as possible, and also use the stems as part of the finished design.

7 Re-assemble the cake. Stand back and then re-arrange anything that looks out of place.

ICELAND POPPY TABLE SETTING

It can be quite a fun idea to use sugar flowers to decorate various items for a wedding reception. The Iceland poppy with its long stems makes an ideal choice. Here I have used Iceland poppies to decorate a glass, napkin and plate. However, these pieces can be time-consuming, so they could be used for perhaps only the wedding couple or for the bride and groom's mothers, or if time and money are not an issue, then for everybody!

FLOWERS FOR THE PLATE, NAPKIN AND GLASS

4 Iceland poppies
(see page 107)
2 buds

EQUIPMENT

Nile green floristry tape
Pliers
Wire cutters
Plate
Napkin
Wine glass

PLATE AND NAPKIN DECORATION

1 Tape together 1 bud, 1 half open, 1 nearly open and 1 fully open Iceland poppy, using ½-width floristry tape. Tuck the stems behind the plate and then attractively bend part of their stems and heads on to the plate.

2 Curl and then wrap the stem of a poppy bud around a folded napkin. Place on top of the plate.

3 Bend the stem on the fully open poppy and curl the base of the wire round. Tuck underneath the napkin, making sure that the flower head is steady.

4 Wrap a fully open poppy stem attractively around the stem of the wine glass.

ICELAND POPPY

The original colour of the Iceland poppy (*Papaver nudicaule*) was yellow; there are now many cultivars in all shades of yellow, white, salmon pink, orange and red. There are no leaves on the stems themselves, only at the base of the plant and, because of this, the leaves are rarely used. They are available from the florist in April to August and once in water can last for up to nine days! In the past, I have used Iceland poppies with montbretia, roses and virginia creeper in a bridal bouquet to wonderful effect.

OVARY

1 Roll a small ball of green flower paste into a cone shape. Tape over a length of 20-gauge wire, moisten the end with egg white and insert into the fine end of the cone. Pinch the pointed base of the cone to secure it in place and flatten the top. Cover the cone with a plastic bag to stop the surface of the paste drying out before the next stage.

2 Roll out a small amount of white paste thinly and cut out a daisy shape using the small daisy cutter. You will find it easier if the paste sticks to the cutter, as you can then simply press the cutter (with the paste inside) on top of the ovary. As the paste is still soft, the daisy shape should be released from the cutter and adhered to the top of the cone. Using a pair of angled tweezers, re-emphasize the shape of the daisy if needed. Dust the green part of the ovary with moss green and the daisy shape with a mixture of primrose and lemon.

STAMENS

3 You will need to use approximately half a bunch of seed-head stamens for each flower. (I have tried other less expensive materials to create the stamens but the seed-head stamens give far more interest!) I also find that because of the amount of stamens required, it is better to use a non-toxic craft glue to stick the stamens around the ovary, other-

MATERIALS

Pale holly/ivy and white flower paste
20 and 28-gauge wires
Small seed-head stamens
Moss green, primrose, lemon and aubergine petal dust (blossom tint)
Mimosa sugartex
Orange and scarlet craft dust

EQUIPMENT

Tiny eight-petal daisy cutter (OP)
Angled tweezers
Non-toxic craft glue
Glue gun and non-toxic glue sticks
Petal templates (see page 158) or poppy cutters (TT)
Sharp scalpel
Asi-es orchid veiner (CC)
Ceramic silk veining tool (HP)
Leaf texturing tool
Nile green floristry tape

wise too much bulk is created behind the flower with the use of floristry tape. (For competition work this is a method that could lose you marks or if the schedule stated no inedible materials other than wire, tape and stamens you would be disqualified. I always feel that for personal use, non-toxic craft glue is acceptable when you consider that both floristry tape and paper covered wire have a certain amount of glue in their makeup.) The ovary must be completely dry before any glue comes into contact with the sugar.

4 First of all, spread the stamens open a little and then apply some glue in a strip across the stamens at the length required. Squeeze the stamens together to make sure that they are all included and then place to one side to allow the glue to dry. Cut the stamens using scissors, apply some glue to the base of the ovary, this time using the glue gun, and wrap the stamens around the ovary quickly before the glue has a chance to dry. Allow to dry thoroughly and then dust the length of each stamen with a mixture of moss green and primrose petal dust. Colour the tips with mixture of primrose and lemon petal dust. To make more mature stamens, paint the tips with egg white and dip into some mimosa sugartex. Using tweezers, bend the stamens open to produce a more realistic effect (if you are making a flower that is not quite fully open, leave the stamens tight around the ovary).

PETALS

5 Very thinly roll out a small amount of white flower paste on a grooved board. Place one of the petal templates on top of the paste and cut out the petal using a sharp scalpel; or use a petal cutter. Remove from the board and insert a moistened 28-gauge white wire into the central ridge.

6 Place the back of the petal on to the orchid veiner and press the surface of the paste with the side of your hand. Remove the petal, turn it over and vein on the upper side. Place the petal down against the board and thin out and frill the top edge using the ceramic silk veining tool and then with a cocktail stick (toothpick). (It does not matter too

much if the edges get torn slightly here and there as this happens to the real poppy petals.) Cup the centre of the petal and allow to dry slightly over some bubble foam. Repeat to make at least one more petal of that size.

7 Repeat this process again, but this time cut out at least two petals using the larger template or cutter. Once you have finished veining and frilling, pinch a ridge on the upper surface of each petal. Allow to dry as before.

Colouring and Assembly

8 It is important to dust the poppy petals while they are still very fresh, so that the vibrant colours can be achieved easily. Dust a patch at the base of each petal on both sides with a mixture of primrose and lemon, then add a small amount of moss green to the very base. The rest of the colouring of the petal is up to you. I am fond of the orange/red poppies and for that I would start by rubbing the orange craft dust into the paste with a brush, leaving the back a touch paler, and then over-dust the edge with scarlet craft dust.

9 Tape the two small petals tightly behind the stamens, and then tape the two larger petals behind the small petals to fill in the gaps. As the petals are still soft, you can re-shape them to give a more realistic finish to the flower. Allow to dry. Steam the flower to remove the dry appearance left by the dusting process.

Buds and Stems

10 Tape over a length of 20-gauge wire several times to thicken the stem. Bend a small open hook on the end, moisten with egg white and attach an egg shaped piece of flower paste in the required size (remember the bud size varies quite a lot). Allow to dry.

11 Roll out some white flower paste very thinly and cut out two or three petals. Vein and frill as for the flower. Apply a little egg white to each petal and arrange on to the dry base. Crumple the petals as you go, as this will help to give it a realistic appearance. Dust the petals with your chosen colours.

Bract

12 Roll out some green flower paste quite thickly and texture the surface with the texturing brush to give the characteristic hairy appearance. Using the small poppy cutter, cut out two bract shapes and hollow out the centre slightly. Apply a little egg white to the underside and attach the two bracts on to either side of the bud or semi-opened flower. Once the bracts are in position, add a little more texture to the surface using a small pair of sharp scissors. Mark a definite indent with a scalpel to divide the two bracts.

13 Dust with moss green, leaving the open edges paler, then over-dust gently with aubergine to accentuate the rough texture. Dust the stems gently with the same colours. Bend the stem into shape. (Real poppy stems are covered with tiny black hairs, fortunately this is not required for sugar work!)

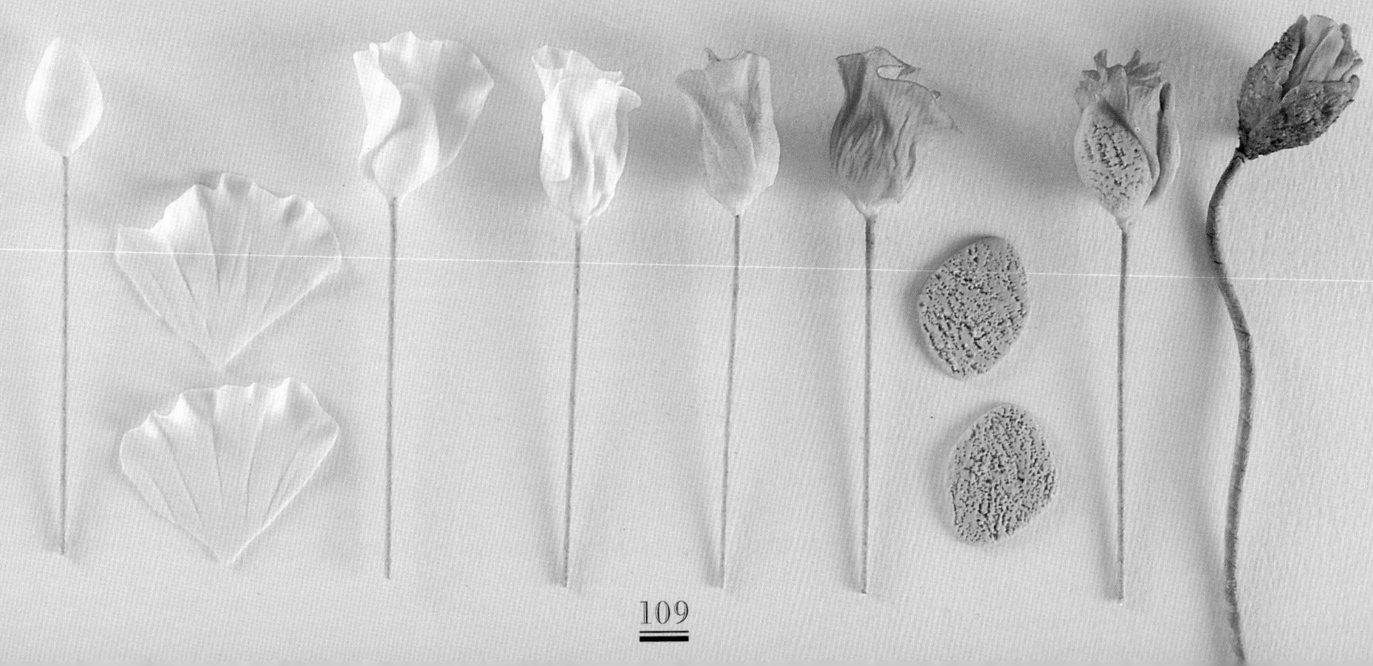

WINTER SOLSTICE WEDDING

Sometimes an impressive centrepiece is requested for a small wedding reception; here is an excellent example of a single-tiered cake displayed to maximum effect with the help of a couple of props and a lavish selection of flowers and foliage – the end result is a dramatic and romantic cake.

MATERIALS

20cm (8 in) heart-shaped cake
Apricot glaze
750g (1½lb) almond paste (marzipan)
Clear alcohol (kirsch or vodka)
1kg (2lb) champagne sugarpaste
Fine green ribbon to trim cake
Green velvet ribbon to trim board
A small amount of flower paste
Holly/ivy, aubergine, plum, primrose and gold petal dust (blossom tint)

EQUIPMENT

Sugarpaste smoothers
28cm (11 in) heart-shaped cake board
Curved leaf cutters (ECC)
Side design template (see page 158)
Quilting wheel (PME)
Fine paintbrush
Nile green floristry tape
Posy pick
Broad green paper ribbon
Long perspex tube stand
Tilting cake stand

FLOWERS

Winter Solstice Free-flowing Posy (see page 113)
Winter Solstice Teardrop-shaped Spray (see page 113)
5 stems of large dark ivy (see page 114)

PREPARATION

1 Brush the cake with apricot glaze and cover with almond paste. Allow to dry overnight. Moisten the almond paste with clear alcohol and cover with champagne sugarpaste, using smoothers to achieve a smooth finish.

2 Cover the cake board with champagne sugarpaste and transfer the cake on top, making sure that you have a neat join between the cake and the board. Allow to dry.

3 Attach a band of fine green ribbon around the base of the cake. Glue a length of green velvet ribbon to the board edge using a glue stick.

SIDE DESIGN

4 Finely roll out some flower paste and cut out two large and four small curved leaves for each section of the design; you will need five sets to complete the cake design. Cover the leaves that you are not working on with a plastic bag to prevent drying . Moisten the back of each of the leaves with clear alcohol and attach to the cake starting with the point of the heart shape, following the template design on page 158.

5 Using the quilting wheel, run a line of stitch marks down the centre of each of the leaves. Dilute a small amount of holly/ivy petal dust with alcohol and, using a fine paintbrush and firm brush strokes, colour in the leaf shapes from the base fading towards the centre. Using the same brush and colour, paint in the trailing green leaf stem and add a couple of small painted leaves to the design. Clean the brush. Dilute some aubergine and plum petal dust, and paint in the remainder of each of the paste leaves and also add the dotted flower arrangement to both sides of the main design. Allow to dry.

6 Mix a small amount of holly/ivy with a dash of primrose and dust in the heart of the design to soften the whole appearance. Apply a little gold petal dust over the top of the paint work on the paste leaves.

ASSEMBLY

7 Wire up the flowers for the sprays (see page 113), taping together with floristry tape, creating a handle. Insert the handle of the teardrop-shaped spray into a posy pick and then into the top left hand corner of the cake.

8 Insert the green paper ribbon through the centre of the long perspex tube stand. Wrap the remainder around the outside using a small piece of double-sided sticky tape at the base to hold it in place. Insert the free-flowing posy into the top of the tube. Adjust the stems a little if needed. Place the cake on to the tilting cake stand using double-sided carpet tape to secure. Place the cake next to the tall floral display and then arrange the extra ivy around the base of the cake and arrangement.

WINTER SOLSTICE SPRAYS

The flowers used in the free-flowing spray have been taped together to form a very unstructured and natural display. It is based on a tussie-mussie shape to begin with, but has a few stems that trail beyond the basic posy shape (there are no strict rules to this type of bouquet). The smaller spray has been formed into a teardrop shape to fit in with the curve of the heart-shaped cake.

FREE-FLOWING POSY (TOP)

3 stems of small eucalyptus and
3 stems of large eucalyptus (see page 120)
2 stems of ivy (see page 114)
1 full apricot-tinged rose, 1 half rose and 4 rosebuds (see page 136)
2 cream half roses (see page 136)
2 sets of rose leaves (see page 138)
1 stem of cream dendrobium orchids, plus one extra flower (see page 116)
5 burgundy hellebores,
3 hellebore buds and 2 sets of hellebore foliage (see page 115)

TEARDROP-SHAPED SPRAY

1 stem of cream dendrobium orchids
2 pieces of small eucalyptus and
1 piece of large eucalyptus
2 stems of ivy
1 full apricot-tinged rose, 1 half rose and 1 rosebud
2 sets of rose leaves
2 hellebores and 2 hellebore buds

EQUIPMENT

20-gauge wires
Nile green floristry tape
Pliers and wire cutters

PREPARATION

1 Strengthen any of the stems that need extra support or length, taping in 20-gauge wires using ½-width nile green floristry tape.

FREE-FLOWING POSY

2 Tape together the foliage first of all, forming a loose posy shape (with a few extra long pieces), bending each of the stems to an angle of 90 degrees. Tape them together using ½-width floristry tape. This will form the handle to the spray.

3 Add the full rose in the centre of the spray – this will form the focal point. It should be slightly higher than any of the other flowers. Continue to add the other half roses and rosebuds (usually these would be placed fairly evenly around the posy, but in this case make them irregular).

4 Add and tape in the dendrobium orchids and hellebores to complete the spray. Cut off any excess wire from the handle to cut down on the bulk and then tape over with full-width floristry tape to neaten.

TEARDROP-SHAPED SPRAY

5 For the teardrop-shaped spray, start the spray with a single stem of dendrobium orchids, a stem of eucalyptus and a stem of trailing ivy.

6 Next, for the basic outline, use the various types of foliage. Tape the stems together at one point to form a handle as described in Step 2.

7 Tape in the roses, positioning the full rose at the focal point of the spray. Fill in the gaps with the hellebore flowers and any extra foliage.

IVY

Ivy (*hedera*) is the most useful form of foliage for the sugar flower maker, as there are many different shapes, shades of green and sizes. It is sometimes thought however to be unlucky for brides to carry ivy in their bouquets – a theory that is totally unfounded, as it is used to symbolize fidelity.

LEAVES

1 Roll out some green flower paste on to a grooved board. The thickness of the paste will depend upon the size of the leaf you are making. Cut out as many leaves as possible from one strip of paste. Cover the leaves that you are not working on to stop the paste drying out.

2 Insert a 24 or 26-gauge wire into the central ridge. Try to insert the wire into at least half the length of the leaf.

3 Vein the leaf using your chosen veiner; the large one pictured has been veined with the large nasturtium leaf veiners.

4 Soften the edges of the leaf using the rounded end of a large celstick. Allow to dry a little before dusting. Tape over each stem with nile green floristry tape.

COLOURING

5 Dust with holly/ivy petal dust on both sides of the leaf, making the back slightly paler. Over dust the upper surface with the dark green mixture. For variation, dust the edges with aubergine or plum petal dust or a mixture of the two. Allow to dry overnight.

6 Dip into ½ glaze, shake off the excess and allow to dry. To create the paler veins, support the leaf from behind with a finger and, using a scalpel, etch off the colour and part of the sugar to show up the paler base colour. Start with the main veins, and then work on the finer ones to complete the leaf.

ASSEMBLY

7 Tape over the end of a 24-gauge wire with ½-width beige floristry tape. Curl the end around a celstick to form a start to the stem (this part would usually be made up from young leaves beginning to form). It usually looks best in bouquets if you start with the smaller leaves and gradually work down to the larger ones. (In nature this is not always the case.) You will need to add an 18-gauge wire quite early on to strengthen the stem.

MATERIALS

Pale green flower paste
18, 24, 26 and 28-gauge wires
Holly/ivy, dark green, aubergine and plum petal dust (blossom tint)
½ glaze (see page 151)

EQUIPMENT

Large ivy cutters (J)
Large ivy or large nasturtium leaf veiners
Nile green and beige floristry tape

5 Stems of ivy various lengths
Dust with holly ivy dust on both sides of leaf making back paler
Dust front leaf dark green
Dust edges with Aubergine

ORE

...ed in detail in my last ... but instead of repeating ... give a brief reminder.

MATERIALS

20, 24, 26 and 28-gauge wires
Small white seed-head stamens
Lemon, spring green, plum, aubergine, dark and moss green petal dust (blossom tint)
Pale and mid-green flower paste
½ glaze (see page 151)

EQUIPMENT

Large Christmas rose cutter (282)
Christmas rose veiner (GI)
Small hellebore leaf veiner (GI)

1 The pistil is made with five pieces of twisted green floristry tape. Tape them together on a 24-gauge wire. Tape a reasonable quantity of stamens around the pistil so that the pistil is higher in the centre. Dust the tips of the stamens with lemon petal dust, then dust some spring green in at the base. Colour the pistil tips with plum petal dust.

NECTARY (PETALS)

2 Roll small balls of pale green flower paste into cone shapes. Hollow out the broad end and then thin the edges with the broad end of the dresden tool. Make ten. Attach to the base of the stamens with egg white or softened flower paste. Dust with spring green petal dust.

SEPALS

3 Roll out pale green flower paste on to a grooved board. Cut out five sepals. Insert a 28-gauge wire in at the base, then vein using the Christmas rose veiner. Soften the edges and firm up on a slight curve.

4 Dust while the paste is at the leather hard stage with plum and aubergine petal dust. Steam, then re-dust to a very dark colour.

5 Tape the sepals around the dried centre using ½-width tape. Tape in two 24-gauge wires to lengthen and strengthen the stem.

BRACTS

6 Form a slender teardrop of mid-green flower paste on the end of a 28-gauge wire. Flatten the paste, using the flat side of a veiner, to make it finer. Vein using the hellebore leaf veiner. Soften the edges, then place the bract on the board and create a serrated edge using the fine end of the dresden tool. Make two or three bracts to add to each bud and flower. Dust with dark green and moss. Dust the edge with a little plum and aubergine mixed. Glaze using a ½ glaze and leave to dry. Tape the bracts behind the flower.

BUDS

7 Attach a cone of pale green paste on to a taped, hooked 20-gauge wire. Form five indents on the bud using a cage with five 24-gauge wires. Pinch the paste out from between the wires to thin the paste and represent tepals. Remove the cage, then twist the sections of the bud together to form a neat shape. Dust to match the flower. Add the bracts, then bend and curve the stem. Dust the stem of the flower and bud with aubergine and plum.

LEAVES

8 Using mid-green paste, cut out leaves. Vein using the hellebore or large briar rose leaf veiner. Make the leaf in the usual way, creating a serrated edge with the fine end of the dresden tool.

DENDROBIUM ORCHID

Often called Singapore orchid, this is the most commonly used orchid in bridal bouquets. White and cream are the most popular colours, although they are available in various shades of pink, magenta, purple and green as there are over a 1,000 species of dendrobium orchid. Sometimes this orchid is dyed to a peach, turquoise or bright yellow – the result is a very artificial-looking flower.

COLUMN

1 Roll a small piece of white or pale melon flower paste into a ball and then into a teardrop shape. This teardrop shape should be no longer than the section between the two side sections and the base of the labellum (lip) cutter. Hollow out the inside of the column using the rounded end of a small celstick. Curve slightly.

2 Tape over a ½-length of 22-gauge wire and bend a hook at one end. Hold the hook with pliers and bend to form a ski stick shape. Moisten the end and pull through the centre of the column to embed the hook into the paste. Pinch the outer part of the column between your finger and thumb to form a subtle ridge. Allow to dry.

3 Attach a tiny ball of paste to the front of the column, tucked on to the inner part. Indent the ball in half using a sharp scalpel. This forms the pollinia.

LABELLUM (LIP PETAL)

4 Roll out a piece of paste quite thinly. Cut out one petal using the labellum cutter/veiner. Press the

MATERIALS

White or very pale melon flower paste
18, 22 and 24-gauge white wires
White, primrose and moss green petal dust (blossom tint), plus your chosen colour if you are making a coloured variety

EQUIPMENT

Dendrobium orchid cutters (HH)
White and nile green floristry tape
Sharp scalpel
Thin sponge

paste firmly against the veins in the cutter, clean off the edges and then remove gently from the mould. Place against the board and frill the bottom section of the lip using the double frilling technique and the broad end of the dresden tool.

5 Place the petal on to a pad and soften the edges of the two side sections, using the rounded end of a small celstick. Hollow out and cup these two side sections using the same tool. Turn the petal over and draw down a central vein on the back of the petal to form a ridge on the upper side.

6 Moisten the base and part of the side sections of the petal and attach to the column. Curl the edges back a little and curl the lip to form an attractive shape. The two side sections should not overlap each other (you should be able to see the central part on the back of the column). Allow to dry.

LATERAL PETALS (WING PETALS)

7 Roll out some more paste and cut out two lateral petals. Press into the mould to get the strongest veining possible. Remove from the mould and place on a pad. Soften the edges of the petals (do not frill). Place to one side to allow to dry slightly.

SEPALS

8 The three sepals are cut out as one complete piece, as this is how they are formed on the flower. Roll out the paste, cut out the sepal shape and press firmly into the mould. Remove and place on to a pad. Soften the edges of the sepals using the rounded end of a celstick.

9 Using the fine end of the dresden tool, draw a strong central vein on the two base sepals (the 'legs'). Pinch the tips of the three sepals between your finger and thumb.

ASSEMBLY

10 To attach the petals to the sepals you can use either egg white or softened flower paste. Position the petals in between the dorsal and lateral sepals (they do not overlap at the centre – see photograph).

11 Moisten the central section below the petals, in between the lateral sepals. Thread the dried column and labellum through the sepals in the centre of the junction between the dorsal sepal and lateral petals. Press the dorsal sepal firmly against the back of the column. Pinch the section in between the two lateral sepals around the base of the labellum (you might need to use a little more egg white at this stage). Cut off the excess paste from the base of the sepals.

12 Curve the dorsal sepal back and the two lateral sepals up

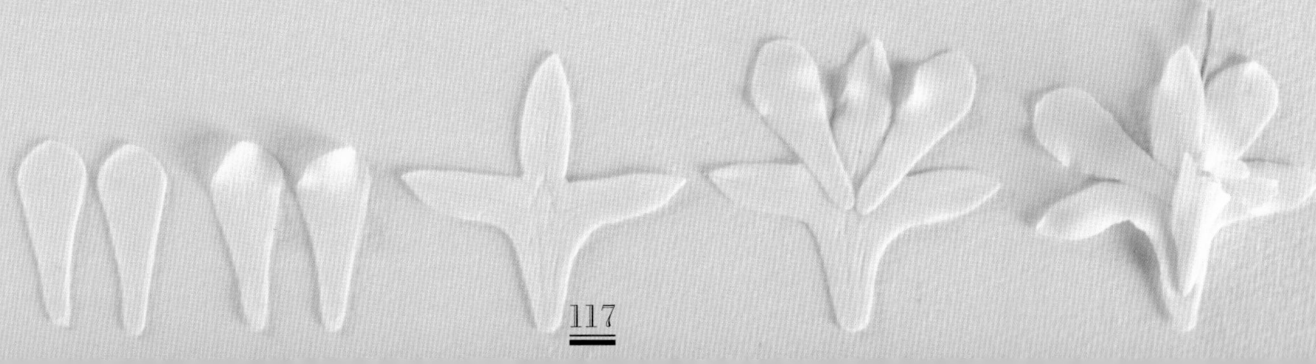

towards the labellum and then curl their tips back.

13 Cut a small square of thin sponge and cut a slit down the centre. Place over the back of the orchid to support the sepals and petals. You might also need to cut two small pieces of sponge to sit behind and support the petals until they are dry.

BUDS

14 The dendrobium orchid bud is quite a difficult shape to replicate. However they always look fine when they are dusted and taped together. They vary between 1-3cm (½ -1¼ in) in length. Roll a ball of flower paste into a teardrop shape. Pinch the tip to a sharp point and curve the teardrop, stroking it at the same time to flatten out one side slightly.

15 Pinch a small spur at the base of the bud and shape between your fingers until it looks complete. The smaller buds often look like small slippers and the larger ones in profile like birds! I suggest that you have to hand a fresh sample as they are not easy to produce without one and even then they are not the simplest of shapes to make. Hook and moisten the end of a 24-gauge wire and insert it into the back of the bud, towards the base. Pinch the paste on to the wire to secure the bud on to the wire. Divide the surface of the bud into three sections using a sharp scalpel to represent the three outer sepals.

COLOURING AND ASSEMBLY

16 Tape over the stem of the flowers and buds with ½-width white tape to thicken each of them. Mix together white, moss and primrose petal dust. Aim the colour at the centre of the flower (the column and centre of the labellum). If the colour is too strong, clean the brush with cornflour (cornstarch), then dust on to the paste. Dust the tips of the sepals and the back of the flower a little stronger.

17 It is best to tape the buds on to the stem and then dust them – this gives more graduation of colour on the stem. Tape a small bud on to the end of an 18-gauge wire. Continue to add the buds down the stem, leaving a little more of each of the short stems a little longer the larger the buds get. Add the flowers, again leaving a reasonable length to each. Dust the main stem and part of each of the shorter stems with the primrose and moss green mixture. Dust the buds with this mixture making the smaller buds much stronger in depth. Steam the whole stem to give a clean, slightly waxy appearance and to seal the colour on to the flowers and buds.

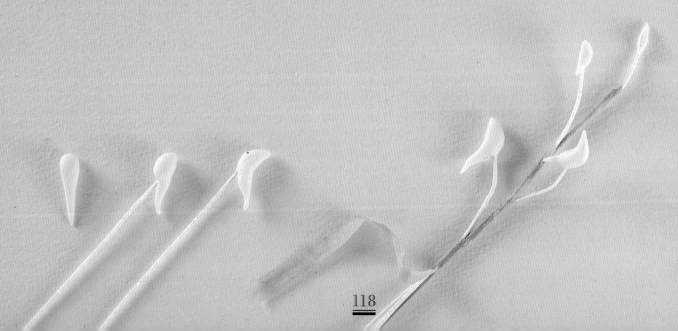

PHOTINIA

It is the new growth of photinia (*Photinia fraseri*) that provides the attractive glossy red leaves over quite a long period of time. Although the plant produces small white flowers in large groups during the spring, it is however usually only the decorative quality of the foliage that is used. I have used some artistic licence with this leaf, reducing the size slightly.

MATERIALS

Pale green flower paste
18, 22 and 26-gauge wires
Plum, aubergine, red, dark green and moss petal dust (blossom tint)
½ and ¾ glaze (see page 151)

EQUIPMENT

Rose leaf cutters (J)
Extra large rose leaf cutter (J)
Large briar rose leaf veiner (GI)
Nile green floristry tape

LEAVES

1 Although these leaves are very red, it is best to start off with a pale green flower paste, then dust them afterwards. Roll out some pale green flower paste on to a grooved board.

2 Cut out leaves of various sizes using the rose leaf cutters. You will need more large leaves to complete a stem. Cut lengths of 26-gauge wire into three lengths. Moisten the end of the wire and insert it into the ridge down the centre of the leaf.

3 Place the leaf between the double-sided briar rose leaf veiner and press firmly. Remove the leaf and place on a pad. Soften the edges of the leaf, working half on the paste and half on the pad, using the rounded end of a large celstick.

COLOURING

4 Dust the leaves while they are still damp. Dust in layers with plum, aubergine, red and add a touch of the greens to the larger leaves. Dip them into either a ½ or ¾ glaze (depending on your own taste), shake off the excess and allow to dry. It is at this stage that the leaves can be reshaped a little before they are allowed to dry.

5 Tape over each stem with ½ width floristry tape, then tape them on to a stronger wire to form a main stem. Tape several stems together to form larger stems of photinia. The leaves also look good when used as individual items in formal sprays, perhaps as an alternative to rose leaves in sprays where roses are dominant. Dust the stems with plum, red and aubergine petal dust.

EUCALYPTUS

Eucalyptus is an ideal foliage for a bride who wants a very soft colour combination. There are many species of eucalyptus available from the florist in different seasons. I prefer the large-leafed forms, as they fill more space and give much more impact.

MATERIALS

Very pale holly/ivy flower paste
20, 26 and 28-gauge wires
Dark green, holly/ivy, white, aubergine, plum and black petal dust (blossom tint)
¼ glaze (see page 151) (optional)

EQUIPMENT

Circle cutters (TT)
Rose petal cutters (TT)
Australian rose petal cutters (TT)
Eucalyptus templates (see page 158)
Fresh eucalyptus leaves or fine large rose leaf veiner
Nile green floristry tape

LEAVES

1 Roll out some pale green flower paste, leaving a thick ridge down the centre. The leaves should not be made too fine. Cut out the shape using your chosen cutter or with a scalpel and the leaf templates on page 158.

2 Cut a length of 26-gauge or 28-gauge wire into five. Moisten one end of a piece of wire and insert it into the central ridge of the leaf. The

wire should be inserted into at least half the length of the leaf. Elongate the leaf if required, simply by stretching the paste between your fingers.

3 Place the leaves on a pad and soften the edges with a large cel-stick. Vein the leaf using either the double-sided rose leaf veiner or preferably with a fresh (or dried) eucalyptus leaf. These leaves tend to be very flat, but I find that drying some with a little curve makes a more attractive finish. You will need to repeat the above process to make a variety of sizes for each stem, remembering that the leaves grow in pairs down the stem.

COLOURING

4 Start colouring the leaves using a flat-headed brush and a little dark green petal dust to add depth to the leaf. Over-dust gently with holly/ivy and a little white petal dust. Dust the edges and the base with aubergine and plum petal dust mixed together. Over-dust with white petal dust heavily. Add a little black petal dust to parts of the leaves if they require more depth. One of the lustre dusts can also be used as an alternative, especially for silver, pearl or Christmas wedding displays.

ASSEMBLY

5 At the top of each eucalyptus stem there are some fine stems, occasionally with tiny leaves attached. The florist usually trims these off. If you would like to add them, simply twist pieces of ¼-width floristry tape back on to itself to form fine strands.

6 Start to tape the stem together by taping a few strands on to the end of a 20-gauge wire using ½-width floristry tape. Start adding the small leaves in pairs and, as you work down the stem, add the medium and then the larger leaves. If you are making a very long stem, you might find that you will need to add an extra 20-gauge wire for strength and to give the overall appearance of more bulk. Smaller stems can be added on to the longer ones to give variation.

7 Dust the main stems with a touch of dark green and a lot of aubergine and plum petal dust. At this final stage you might need to add more white or aubergine on some of the leaves. Bend the whole stem and leaves to give movement to the whole piece.

PEONY WEDDING CAKE

The peony (*Paeonia*) has long been a popular flower for weddings. Here I have used only three flowers to create impact on a very stylish yet simple wedding cake. I have supplied a brush embroidery design on page 157 if a cake side design is preferred.

MATERIALS

20cm (8 in) and 30cm (12 in) long octagonal cakes
Apricot glaze
2kg (4lb) almond paste (marzipan)
Clear alcohol (kirsch or vodka)
3kg (6lb) pale green sugarpaste, using mint and holly/ivy paste food colouring
Fine dusky pink ribbon to trim cakes
Broad dusky pink ribbon to trim boards

EQUIPMENT

Sugarpaste smoothers
20cm (8 in), 28cm (11 in) and 40cm (16 in) long octagonal cake boards
Medium tube stand
2 posy picks

FLOWERS

3 peonies (see page 124)
4 buds
25-35 sets of leaves

PREPARATION

1 Brush both the cakes with apricot glaze and cover with almond paste. Allow to dry overnight. Moisten the almond paste with clear alcohol and cover with pale green sugarpaste, using sugarpaste smoothers to achieve a good finish.

2 Cover the two larger cake boards with pale green sugarpaste. Transfer the cakes on top, making sure you have a neat join between the cake and board.

3 Attach a band of fine dusky pink ribbon around the base of the cakes. Glue a length of broad dusky pink ribbon to the board edges using a non-toxic glue stick.

ASSEMBLY

4 Place the base tier on top of the smallest cake board to lift it up from the table slightly. Place the tube stand directly behind the large cake, then position the smaller cake at a slight angle pointing away from the base tier.

5 Wire up the flowers, bud and foliage, making the larger spray with two flowers, three buds and leaves. Make the other spray with just one peony. Insert a posy pick into each cake and insert the main stem of each of the sprays into them. Place a bud and some foliage towards the back of the base tier on the board to add a little more interest and balance the design.

6 If required, pipe the brush embroidery design on to the sides of the cakes following the template on page 157.

7 The single tier cake shown provides an alternative using only the larger base tier. The three peonies have been used to create a slightly different, more compact design.

PEONY

The peony (*Paeonia*) originates from China where it has been cultivated for over 1000 years. The colour variation is vast, including white, cream, yellow, pink, magenta and burgundy varieties. They are available from the florist from May to July which, being the height of the wedding season, makes them a popular choice. As this is a large, showy flower you won't need to use many to make an amazing impact. The peony described here is based on one of the tree peony varieties.

MATERIALS

Pale green, pale ruby, white and mid-green flower paste
18, 20, 22, 24, 26 and 30-gauge wires
Vine green, aubergine, plum, lemon, primrose, dark green and holly/ivy petal dust (blossom tint)
Deep magenta craft dust
White or lemon small hammer-head stamens
½ glaze (see page 151)

EQUIPMENT

Nile green floristry tape
Large rose petal cutters (TT549,550,551) or templates (see page 157)
Small rose petals (TT276,278,279,280)
Ceramic silk veining tool (HP)
Apple tray or other suitable cupped former
Peony leaf templates (see page 157) or cutters (TT)
Peony leaf veiners (GI)

PISTIL

1 The pistil is made up in three or five sections; it depends how mature the flower is as to the size of the sections. A mature flower can have very large sections forming the

fruit: it is in this form that I prefer to make them. Cut three or five short lengths of 26-gauge wire. Hook and moisten the end. Roll a ball of pale green flower paste into a teardrop shape and insert the wire into the base. Pinch a ridge on one side of the teardrop, and then curl the tip on to the side with the ridge. Repeat this process to make three or five sections. Tape the sections together before they dry, using ½-width nile green tape. Press the separate sections together to form a tight, attractive centre. Allow to dry, then dust with vine green petal dust. Dust the tips with a little deep magenta and aubergine (this varies between the different varieties).

STAMENS

2 The stamens vary a little between the different varieties and also at the various stages of maturity. The anthers are very large to begin with and, as the flower matures, they become very fine. They can be represented with thread or with commercially prepared stamens. I use small hammer-head stamens, as the peony is a large flower and I feel it gives a stronger centre to the flower. Tape approximately 80 (¼–⅓ of a bunch) lemon or white stamens around the fruit, using ½-width tape. Trim off the excess stamens from the base and tape down over the wire.

3 Dust the tips of the stamens with a mixture of lemon and primrose petal dust. Dust the length of each of the stamens with deep magenta craft dust. Using tweezers, bend and curl the stamens to open them slightly. In a flower that has only just opened, the stamens will be very tight together and the ovary not visible. Place to one side.

PETALS

4 Roll out some ruby coloured flower paste, leaving a thick ridge at the centre. The paste should not be too fine or too thick. Squash the three large rose petal cutters into the shape to match the design on page 157 or cut out three templates.

5 Insert a moistened 26-gauge wire in at the base of each of the petals. Place the petal back on to the board and vein both sides using the silk veining tool. Roll the tool across the petal in a fan formation, trying not to alter the shape of the petal too much. Next frill the upper edge of the petal using the silk veining tool. Soften the frill by re-frilling with a cocktail stick (toothpick).

6 Hollow out the centre of each petal, by stretching and stroking the paste between your fingers and thumbs. Place on an apple tray to dry the petals into shape. You will need to cut out at least six medium and nine large petals to complete a flower – more petals will produce a more flamboyant flower.

COLOURING AND ASSEMBLY

7 As there are many different types of peony, the colouring will be very individual. If you want to copy the one pictured, then dust each of the petals from the base with deep magenta craft dust, fading the colour out towards the top edge. Dust a patch of aubergine petal dust at the base.

8 Tape the six smaller petals around the stamens using ½ – width nile green floristry tape. Add the larger petals, in between each of the first layer and then add the remaining petals wherever they are needed. If the petals are still damp, re-shape them to form a more relaxed, realistic effect. Tape an 18-gauge wire alongside the main stem if it needs extra support.

CALYX

9 The calyx is made up from three rounded sepals and two longer narrow sepals. Roll out a strip of pale green paste on to a grooved board and cut out three sizes of rose petal shapes (278, 279, 280). Insert a moistened 30-gauge wire into the thick ridge of each sepal. Place them on a pad and soften the edges. Cup and hollow out the ridged side of each sepal. Pinch a tiny point at the rounded end of the sepal. Allow to firm up a little.

10 To make the two narrow sepals, you can either cut them out with a scalpel or use the quicker method of rolling a sausage of paste on to a 30-gauge wire. Thin the sausage between your fingers and palms and form a neat point at the tip. Place on a board and flatten with the flat side of a veiner. You need to make one sepal slightly longer than the other. Pinch a vein down the centre and allow to firm up. Dust all of the sepals with some vine green petal dust and catch the tips with a mixture of aubergine and plum.

11 Tape the three rounded sepals on to the back of the flower first of all and then add the two narrow sepals so that they are quite evenly spaced.

BUDS

12 Tape over a ½ length of 18-gauge wire using ½-width nile green tape. Bend a large open hook at one end of the wire using pliers. Roll a medium to large sized ball of white paste, moisten the hooked wire and insert into the ball of paste. Pinch the paste on to the wire to secure it in place. Allow to dry completely.

13 Roll out some ruby paste thinly and cut out five or six petals using either rose petal cutter 551 or 276 (this will depend how big the central ball is). Vein and frill as for the flower. Moisten the base of each of the petals and attach them to the dried ball. Start by placing the petals on opposite each other, creasing and pressing down each of the petals as you put them on to create a tight bud.

14 Dust the petals to match the flower. Attach a calyx as for the flower, but this time do not wire the three rounded sepals – they are simply stuck to the base of the bud. Wire the two long sepals and wire them on to the stem. Thicken the stem with some shredded absorbent kitchen paper taped over with ½-width tape. Dust the stem with vine green and then over-dust with aubergine petal dust. Steam the buds and flowers to remove the dry appearance left by the dusting process.

LEAVES

15 The leaves grow in sets of three. There are a number of leaf templates on page 157. Some of the shapes are interchangeable and you will need a lot of foliage to complete a flower stem. Roll out some mid-green flower paste, leaving a thick ridge down the centre. Place a leaf template on top of the paste and cut out the leaf using a sharp scalpel. Insert a moistened 26-gauge or 24-gauge wire, depending on the size of the leaf, into the thick ridge so that it supports at least half the length of the leaf.

16 Vein the leaf using the peony leaf veiners. Place on a pad and soften the edges to take away the harsh cut edge. Pinch down the central veins (if the leaf is tri-lobed, then pinch each of the sections). Allow the leaves to firm up fairly flat but with a slight curve at the ends. Repeat to make a complete set of leaves.

COLOURING AND ASSEMBLY

17 Dust the leaves with vine green, dark green and holly/ivy petal dust. Dust the edges of the leaves with plum and aubergine. Dip into a ½ glaze. Dry. Tape the leaves together into sets of three. If the leaves are large, tape a 22-gauge or 20-gauge wire on to the stem.

18 Tape two or three sets of leaves on to each of the flower and bud stems. Join two bud stems together and add another set of leaves at the axil. Add the flowers and leaves, adding a set of leaves at the join between the two stems. Dust the stems with aubergine.

AUTUMN HAZE

Autumn provides the sugarcrafter with the ideal opportunity to use some of nature's very rich colouring. This one-tier cake includes a vibrant selection of warm colours using the ever popular rose with some of the more unusual flowers, such as Guernsey lily or nerine and shining euphorbia, to make a stunning centrepiece.

MATERIALS

25cm (10 in) pointed oval cake
Apricot glaze
1kg (2lb) almond paste (marzipan)
Clear alcohol (kirsch or vodka)
1.5kg (3lb) sugarpaste
Nasturtium and poppy paste food colouring
Orange ribbon and 'S' scroll gold braiding to trim cake
Broad burnt orange ribbon to trim board

EQUIPMENT

Sugarpaste smoothers
36cm (14 in) pointed oval cake board
Florists' staysoft
Small perspex disc (HP)

FLOWERS

Autumn Haze Curved Arrangement (see page 131)
1 Ranunculus (see page 72)

PREPARATION

1 Colour the sugarpaste with nasturtium and poppy paste colouring and allow to rest before handling again.

2 Brush the cake with apricot glaze and cover with almond paste. Leave to dry overnight. Moisten the surface of the almond paste with clear alcohol and cover with the pale orange sugarpaste, using sugarpaste smoothers and the pad technique (see page 94) to achieve a good finish. Cover the board with the pale orange sugarpaste. Transfer the cake on to it, in a slightly off-set position. Make sure there is a neat join between the base of the cake and the board. Allow to dry.

3 Attach two bands of orange ribbon (or one slightly broader ribbon) around the base of the cake. Position a band of the gold braiding over the top of the orange ribbon. Place a length of broad burnt orange ribbon around the cake board edge, attaching with non-toxic glue stick.

ASSEMBLY

4 Place a clump of florists' staysoft on to the small perspex disc. Arrange the flowers and foliage for the Autumn Haze Curved Arrangement into the staysoft as instructed on page 131. Place the arrangement on top of the cake. Add one single ranunculus at the base of the cake slightly underneath the arrangement.

AUTUMN HAZE CURVED ARRANGEMENT

You will find that with this type of arrangement it is better to arrange the flowers directly on to the cake; however you will need to be careful not to mark the sugarpaste as you do so, otherwise the arrangement will have to be re-designed to cover the error! This is often the way new floral designs are created.

FLOWERS

1 long stem of shining euphorbia with foliage and 2 short stems without foliage (see page 134)
1 full rose, 3 half roses and 1 rosebud (see page 136)
1 stem of red Guernsey lily with three flowers (see page 132)
3 sets of rose leaves (see page 139)
3 stems of hypericum berries (see page 78)
5 ranunculus, various sizes (see page 72)
5 photinia leaves (see page 119)

EQUIPMENT

Florists' staysoft
1 small oval acrylic base (HP)
Fine pliers
Wire cutters

PREPARATION

1 Attach a clump of staysoft to the acrylic base (as this arrangement is not too large there is no need to glue the two together). Hook the ends of each of the flower stems in turn, once they have been cut to the required size.

ASSEMBLY

2 Insert the three stems of shining euphorbia into the staysoft to form the first basic curves to the arrangement.

3 Add the large rose at the centre of the arrangement to form the focal point. Add the other roses around the main flower. Position the Guernsey lilies at the back of the arrangement, to the right hand side of the large rose. Insert the two sets of rose leaves opposite one another, either side of the large rose.

4 Next insert the three stems of hypericum, evenly spaced around the arrangement. Fill in the gaps with the various sizes of ranunculus. To add depth to the display, insert the five photinia leaves.

5 Finally, stand back from the cake and the arrangement to take another look to check to see if any of the flowers need re-positioning or relaxing.

GUERNSEY LILY

Originally from South Africa, the Guernsey lily (*Nerine sarniensis*) is a descendant of bulbs from a South African ship stranded on Guernsey. The flower that I have made is one of the red-flowering hybrids. There are also, on a limited scale, orange, salmon, pink and cerise flowers. Other varieties have provided the more popular bright pink flowers.

MATERIALS

18, 24, 28 and 33-gauge white wires
Poppy and green flower paste
Aubergine, deep purple, white, vine green, moss green, cream and nutkin brown petal dust (blossom tint)
Scarlet craft dust

EQUIPMENT

Cattleya orchid sepal cutter (TT8) or template (see page 156)
Nile green floristry tape

STAMENS

1 Cut six short lengths of 33-gauge white wire. Bend a closed hook in one end of each wire. Hold the hook at its centre with pliers and bend it into a 'T' bar shape.

2 Attach a tiny sausage of paste on to each 'T' bar shape (without egg white) to form the anther, which should be a neat shape. Dust the filament with scarlet craft dust and the anthers with aubergine and deep purple petal dust. If making a mature flower, dot the anther with white petal dust to represent pollen.

3 Tape the six stamens together, leaving three of them longer in length. (The pistil is shorter than the stamens and is not essential to include.) However if you choose to do so, simply add an extra 33-gauge scarlet dusted wire. It is only in a very mature flower that the pistil is very prominent and the tip divided into three curled sections (this would then be made with floristry tape). Curl the group of stamens slightly.

PETALS

4 Roll out poppy coloured flower paste on to a fine grooved board. Squash the cattleya sepal cutter to make a slimmer petal shape. With a sharp scalpel, cut out six petals using the template or orchid cutter. Insert a moistened 28-gauge wire into the central ridge of each petal.

5 Place each petal in turn on to the board and frill the sides of the

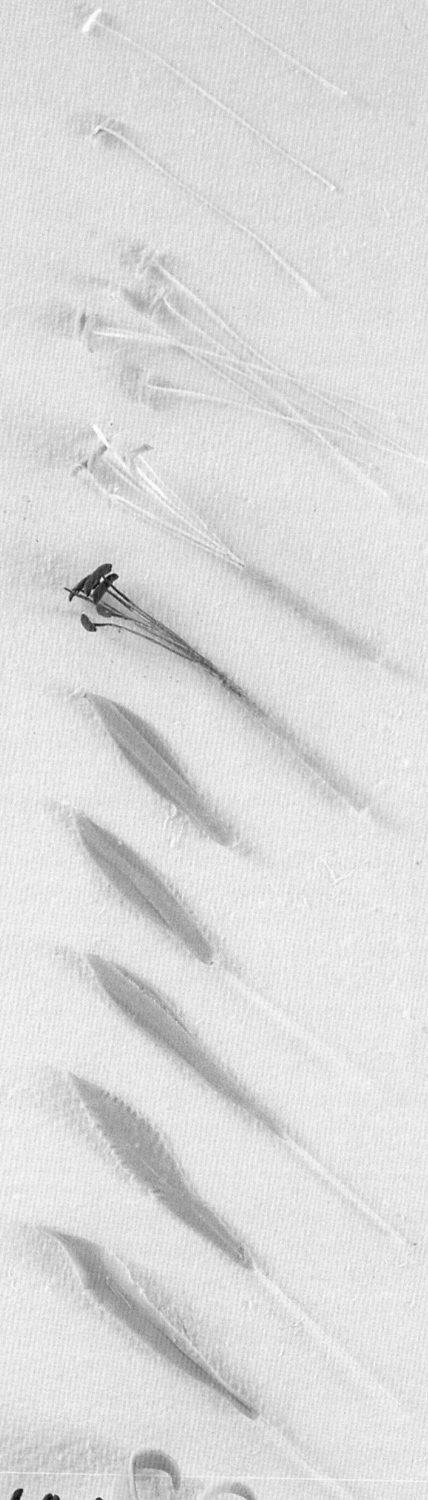

petal, using the broad end of the dresden tool to double frill the edge. Place each petal on to a pad and, using the fine end of the tool, draw down a central vein on the upper surface. Curl into shape and allow to firm up a little, drying on their sides.

6 Dust each petal with scarlet craft dust, leaving the central part pale to allow the base colour to show through. If necessary, dust the centre with a little white petal dust. Tape three of the petals around the stamens and then tape the remaining three in between each of the first layer, slightly recessed. If the petals are still wet, you should now be able to re-curl the edges if needed.

OVARY

7 Attach a ball of green flower paste at the base of the flower. Divide the ovary into three sections using a scalpel. Dust with vine green petal dust and a touch of moss.

BUDS

8 The buds are long and slender in shape. Using poppy coloured flower paste, insert a 24-gauge wire, hooked in at the base. Divide the length of each into three sections using a cage made from three 28-gauge wires. Add the ovary as for the flower. Dust with scarlet craft dust. The number of buds vary from stem to stem, so the choice is entirely up to the individual.

ASSEMBLY

9 Tape together a group of buds and two to three flowers on to an 18-gauge wire using ½-width floristry tape. Add a couple more wires to strengthen the stem if the flowers are to be used in an arrangement. Thicken the stem with shredded absorbent kitchen paper and then tape over the top. Dust the stem with vine and moss green.

10 Where the flowers and buds join the main stem, there are some stringy bits and two bracts. The stringy bits can be made with either some thread dusted with a touch of cream or with the stringy bits at the base of a fresh corn on the cob husk. Simply tape them on to the stem and curl some of them back slightly. To form the bracts, either cut out two shapes using white flower paste or floristry tape. Try to give these pieces a distressed, crumpled appearance. Dust with cream and nutkin brown petal dust and tape on the stem. Re-dust the stem if needed.

NOTE

To make the more popular pink variety of nerine, colour the flower paste with a small amount of ruby paste colour. Dust with fuchsia, plum and deep purple petal dust. The anthers are coloured only for the red variety, but the filaments should be dusted to a strong pink instead of red. These flowers tend to be larger that the red type, although there are some varieties with very small, fine flowers.

SHINING EUPHORBIA

Shining euphorbia (*Euphorbia fulgens*) is a shrub that originates from Mexico and is part of the family of plants that includes the ever popular poinsettia (*Euphorbia pulcherrima*). Like the poinsettia, shining euphorbia is used for the ornamental quality of the brightly coloured bracts (its flowers look very much like stamens at the centre of the flower-like bracts). The original colour was orange, but there are now many hybrid forms in white, cream, yellow, salmon pink and a deep orange/red. The long stems that are characteristic of this plant look wonderful in bridal bouquets. The leaves have a tendency to drop naturally (this does not indicate that the plant is past its best), and sometimes the florist will remove the leaves to form a neater stem for use in bridal work.

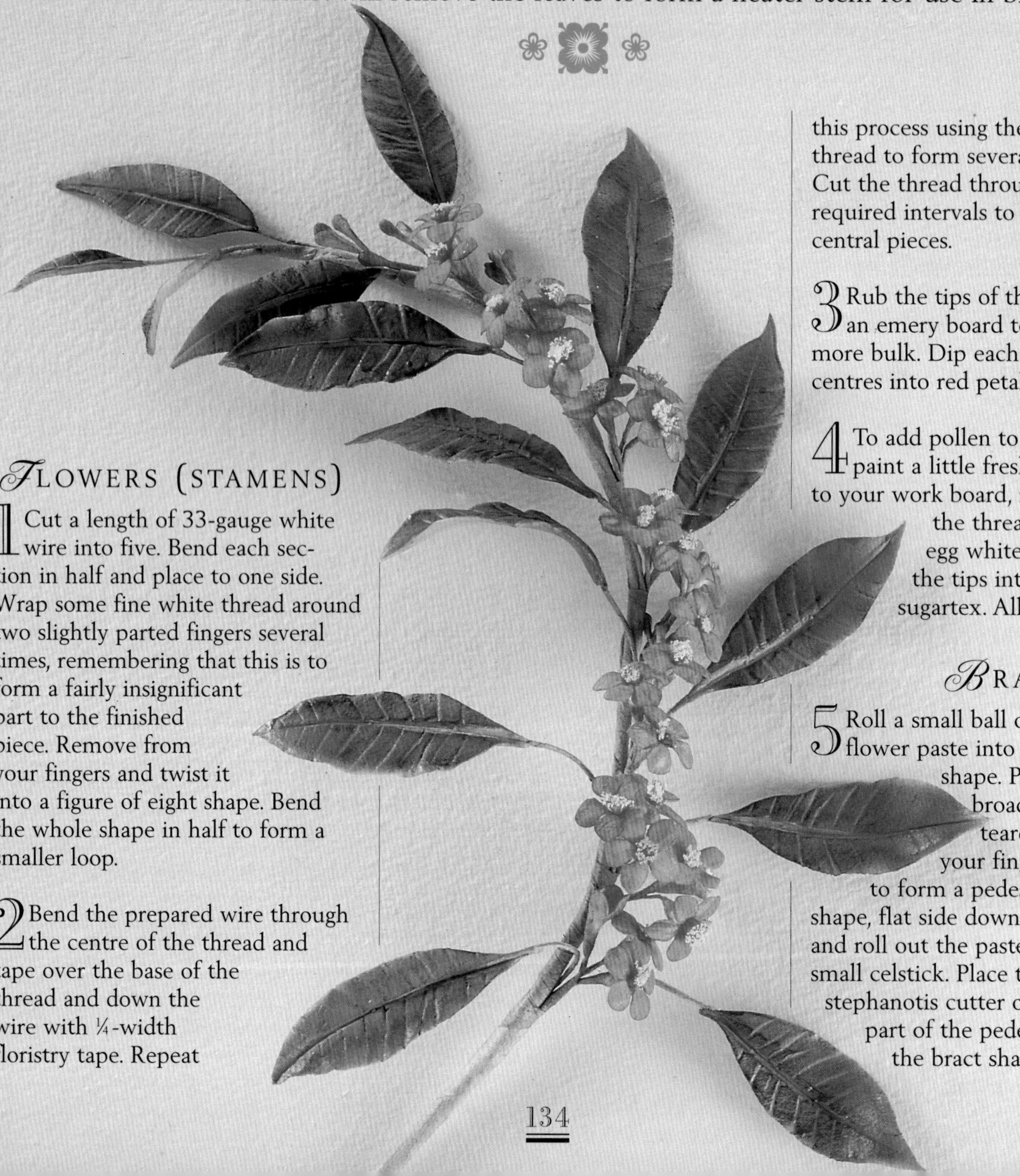

FLOWERS (STAMENS)

1 Cut a length of 33-gauge white wire into five. Bend each section in half and place to one side. Wrap some fine white thread around two slightly parted fingers several times, remembering that this is to form a fairly insignificant part to the finished piece. Remove from your fingers and twist it into a figure of eight shape. Bend the whole shape in half to form a smaller loop.

2 Bend the prepared wire through the centre of the thread and tape over the base of the thread and down the wire with ¼-width floristry tape. Repeat this process using the same loop of thread to form several short lengths. Cut the thread through at the required intervals to form separate central pieces.

3 Rub the tips of the thread against an emery board to give the tips more bulk. Dip each of the thread centres into red petal dust.

4 To add pollen to the flowers, paint a little fresh egg white on to your work board, rub the tips of the thread gently in the egg white and then dip the tips into some mimosa sugartex. Allow to dry.

BRACTS

5 Roll a small ball of pale melon flower paste into a teardrop shape. Pinch out the broad end of the teardrop between your fingers and thumbs to form a pedestal. Place the shape, flat side down, on your board and roll out the paste finely using a small celstick. Place the small stephanotis cutter over the thick part of the pedestal and cut out the bract shape. Rub your

MATERIALS

20, 26, 28 and 33-gauge wires
Fine cotton lace-making thread (Brock 120)
Red, tangerine, holly/ivy, dark green and white petal dust (blossom tint)
Mimosa sugartex
Pale melon or white and mid-holly/ivy flower paste
Clear alcohol (kirsch or vodka)
¼ glaze (see page 151)

EQUIPMENT

Nile green floristry tape
Small stephanotis cutter (TT568)
Poinsettia cutters (J)
Poinsettia leaf veiners (GI)
Fine paintbrush

thumb over the cutter before removing the paste to make sure that you have clean cut edges to the shape.

6 Place the shape, flat side down, on to the board. Using the small celstick again, roll and broaden each of the five sections. Place the shape on to a pad and hollow out the back of each of the sections using the rounded end of the celstick.

7 Using the pointed end of the celstick, open up the centre of the bract shape. Moisten the base of the thread flower centre and pull through the centre of the bract shape. Allow to firm up a little before colouring. Repeat the process to make a large number of flowers.

BUDS

8 Bend a small hook on to the end of a very short piece of 33-gauge wire. Roll a small cone shaped piece of melon flower paste and insert the hooked wire into the fine end of the cone. Divide the rounded end into five sections using a cage made with five pieces of 33-gauge wire.

LEAVES

9 Roll out mid holly/ivy flower paste on to a grooved board. Cut out several leaves using the various sizes of poinsettia cutters (use the plainer cutters in the set). Insert a moistened 28-gauge or 26-gauge wire into the central ridge of each leaf.

10 Vein using the poinsettia leaf veiners. Place the leaves on to a pad and soften the edges. Pinch the central vein on the back of each leaf to emphasize the vein. Allow to firm up before dusting.

COLOURING AND ASSEMBLY

11 Dust each of the bracts with tangerine and over-dust with red petal dust. The back of the bracts should be paler and the tube should be left cream. Dust the base of the tube with a touch of green. Dust the tips of the buds to match the flowers. Tape the flowers and buds into the mixed groups of three.

12 Dust the leaves with holly/ivy and dark green petal dust. Mix together a small amount of alcohol with white petal dust and a touch of green. Using a fine paintbrush, paint in the central vein fading out towards the tip, then paint in a few of the finer veins at the base of the leaf. Allow to dry. Dip into a ¼ glaze, shake off the excess and dry.

13 To form a stem, tape a small leaf on to the end of a 20-gauge wire, leaving part of its stem showing. Continue to tape down the stem adding leaves, graduating in size and alternating from left to right. Start to add the bracts at intervals down the stem, adding a single leaf to each group until you have completed the length of stem required. Dust the main stem with dark green and holly/ivy green. Bend the complete stem into its arching shape. Steam the whole piece.

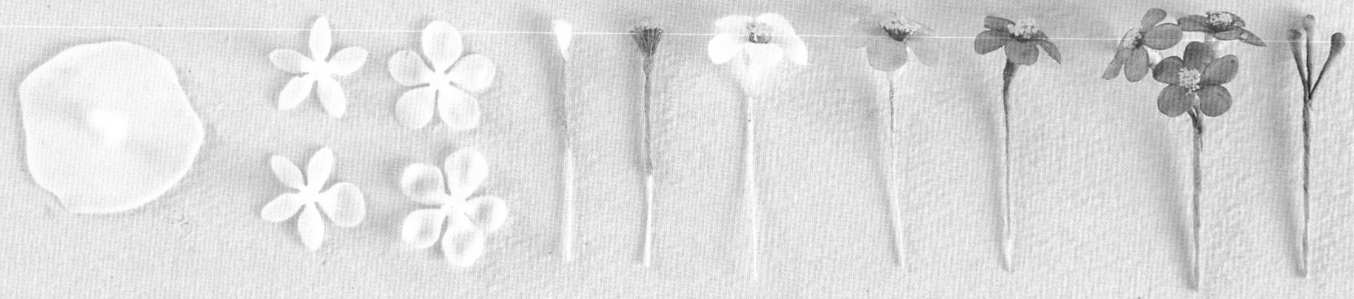

ROSE

Roses (*Rosa*) are still by far the most popular and most loved flower in the world. Commercial roses can be divided into four main groups - large, medium, small and spray roses.

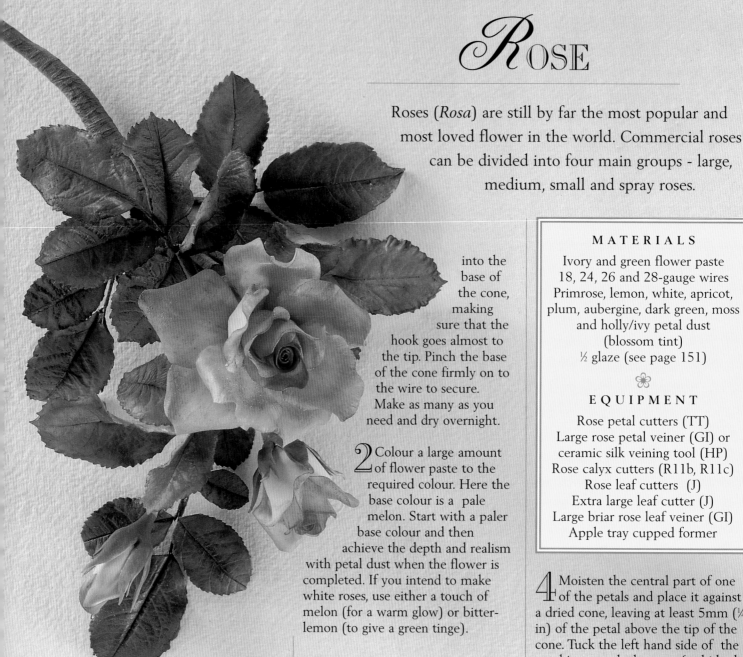

MATERIALS

Ivory and green flower paste
18, 24, 26 and 28-gauge wires
Primrose, lemon, white, apricot, plum, aubergine, dark green, moss and holly/ivy petal dust (blossom tint)
½ glaze (see page 151)

EQUIPMENT

Rose petal cutters (TT)
Large rose petal veiner (GI) or ceramic silk veining tool (HP)
Rose calyx cutters (R11b, R11c)
Rose leaf cutters (J)
Extra large leaf cutter (J)
Large briar rose leaf veiner (GI)
Apple tray cupped former

PREPARATION

1 Roll a ball of white flower paste into a cone with a sharp point and a fairly broad base. (It should measure no longer than the small rose petal cutter you are planning to use; for a bud it should be quite a lot smaller.) Tape over a half length of 18-gauge wire and bend an open hook in the end using pliers. Moisten the wire with egg white and insert it into the base of the cone, making sure that the hook goes almost to the tip. Pinch the base of the cone firmly on to the wire to secure. Make as many as you need and dry overnight.

2 Colour a large amount of flower paste to the required colour. Here the base colour is a pale melon. Start with a paler base colour and then achieve the depth and realism with petal dust when the flower is completed. If you intend to make white roses, use either a touch of melon (for a warm glow) or bitter-lemon (to give a green tinge).

FIRST AND SECOND LAYERS

3 Roll out some coloured flower paste thinly, and cut out four petals using the smaller rose petal cutter. Place the petals on a pad and soften the edges using the rounded end of a large celstick, working half on the paste and half on the pad. If you work with the tool too much on the inner edge, the petal will curl up and form an unattractive shape. Do not frill the edges of the petals, simply soften the harsh cut edge.

4 Moisten the central part of one of the petals and place it against a dried cone, leaving at least 5mm (¼ in) of the petal above the tip of the cone. Tuck the left hand side of the petal in towards the cone (to hide the tip of the cone completely). Wrap the other side of the petal around to form a tight spiral, leaving the end slightly open. Do not worry about the base of the cone at this stage, concentrate only on the formation of the petals from an overhead view.

5 Moisten the bases of the remaining three petals. Tuck the first of these underneath the open edge of the petal on the cone, the second underneath the first and the third underneath the second. The petals

should now be fairly evenly spaced. Moisten the petals if needed and close them all tight, pulling the petals down at an angle rather than wrapping them straight around. There are now enough petals on the cone to make a small bud, but for a larger rose, open up one of the petals again.

THIRD AND FOURTH LAYERS

6 Roll out some more paste and cut out another three petals using the same size cutter as before. Soften the edges of each of the petals, then vein using either the double sided veiner or the silk veining tool or a combination of the two. If you are making smaller roses then you do not need to worry too much about veining. Moisten the base of each of the petals again, tuck the first petal of the third layer underneath the last petal of the second layer. Continue to add the remaining petals as before, this time pinching a very gentle central vein on each of the petals between your finger and thumb as you add them to the rose.

7 Cut out another three petals and repeat Step 6, this time wrapping the petals less tightly.

FIFTH AND SIXTH LAYERS

8 Roll out more paste and cut another three petals using the slightly larger petal cutter. Vein and soften each of the petals as before. Cup the centre of each petal using the rounded end of a large celstick.

9 Moisten the base of each petal and attach them as before, making sure that the centre of each covers a join in the previous layer. The rose should now be quite open; curl back the petal edges using your fingers or a cocktail stick (toothpick). This rose is termed a 'half rose'; I use more half roses than full ones in a spray or bouquet.

10 The sixth layer can either follow on as before or the petals can be wired individually. Roll out a small piece of paste leaving a thick ridge down the centre (this needs to be very subtle). Cut out the petal using same size cutter as before. Hook and moisten the end of

a 26-gauge wire. Insert into only the base of the thick ridge. Soften the edges and place into the veiner. Remove from the veiner and stroke the centre of the petal to stretch it and cup it slightly. Place into an apple tray former to firm up. Repeat to make eight to ten petals. Curl the edges back a little at this stage.

ASSEMBLY AND COLOURING

11 I usually tape the petals around the rose centre and then petal dust them as I find that I end up with a more balanced result. Mix together some primrose, lemon and white petal dust. Dust in at the base of each petal on the inside and slightly heavier on the back. Next, mix together the selected main colour; here I am using a mixture of apricot and plum petal dust. Start by dusting the centre of the rose, firmly and quite strong in colour. Gradually dust the outer petals starting at the edges and fading down to the base. Steam and re-dust if necessary.

CALYX

12 Roll a ball of mid-green flower paste into a cone and pinch out the base to form a hat shape. Using a small celstick, roll out the base to make it a little thinner, although the calyx should have quite a 'fleshy' appearance. Cut out the calyx, and elongate each sepal by rolling with the celstick.

13 Place the calyx cutter on a pad and cup the inner part of each of the sepals. Dust the inner calyx with a mixture of white and moss green to make it paler. If wished, make some fine cuts in the edges of each sepal with a pair of fine scissors, to give them a 'hairy' appearance. The number of cuts on a florists' rose vary and some have no cuts at all; only a wild rose has an exact number of hairs/cuts on each sepal.

14 Moisten the centre of the calyx and attach it to the back of the rose or bud, positioning each sepal so that it covers a join between two outer petals. On a full-blown rose, the calyx would curl right back and on a rosebud it would be tight around the bud. For a competition, where the sepals should curl right back, then attach the calyx just before you wire them into a spray. This will enable the sepals to move around comfortably, and dry in position. Dust the outer part of the calyx with dark green and moss. Keep the very edges of each sepal much paler. Some roses benefit from a touch of plum, red or aubergine to the tips of the sepals. Dry; paint the sepals with a ¼ or ½ glaze (optional).

LEAVES

15 Rose leaves are not used as a main foliage in bridal bouquets and sprays. They are however essential in arrangements and if you

are making roses to display in a vase. I occasionally incorporate a few stems into a spray or bouquet, especially if I am running short of other foliage and have rose leaves spare. Rose leaves on commercial florists' roses can grow in sets of three or five, depending upon the variety. Roll out some mid-green paste, leaving a thick ridge down the centre (a grooved board may be used for this). Cut out a selection of sizes using rose leaf cutters; the quality of rose leaf cutters varies a lot – avoid at all costs any metal rose leaf cutters. You will need one large, two medium and two small leaves per stem.

16 Choose lengths of 26-gauge or 28-gauge wire (depending on the size of the leaf), and cut into four. Moisten one end of each wire and insert into the thick ridge of a leaf. The wire should be inserted into at least half the length of the leaf. Vein the leaf using the briar rose leaf veiner. Place the leaf on a pad and soften the edges using a large celstick. Pinch a vein down the centre of the leaf and shape the leaf between your finger and thumb to give a little more movement.

17 Using a flat brush, dust the back of each leaf with white and a touch of moss green petal dust. Over-dust with plum and aubergine on the edges and bring a little of the colour down on to the veins (not all roses have this colouring). Turn the leaf over and dust the edges and one side heavier with the aubergine and plum mixture. Dust the upper side of the leaf with dark green and then over-dust with either holly/ivy or moss green. Dip into a ½ glaze, shake off the excess and allow to dry.

ASSEMBLY

18 Tape the leaves together into groups of three or five, starting with a large leaf, then the medium leaves, and finishing with the two small leaves.

NOTE

If you have to make a few roses in a hurry and do not have any pre-dried centres, then try this alternative method. Hook an uncovered 18-gauge wire, make the cone as before and then, using a cigarette lighter or gas hob, heat the hook until it is red hot. Quickly insert the hook into the rose cone, neaten the base and allow to firm a little. The sugar caramelizes, cools quickly and gives a secure base (if you use moisture it tends to slide around during the making of a rose).

GROOM'S CAKE

A groom's cake is an excellent choice for a wedding where the groom, or the bride (and perhaps some of the guests) does not like fruit cake. This cake would perhaps be a chocolate, carrot, Madeira or orange sponge cake in place of the traditional fruit cake. The decoration can be novelty or a floral combination of more masculine flowers to tie in with the main colour scheme.

MATERIALS

25cm (10 in) kidney-shaped cake
Apricot glaze
1kg (2lb) almond paste (marzipan)
Clear alcohol (kirsch or vodka)
1.5kg (3lb) white sugarpaste
Yellow and willow green ribbon
Green velvet ribbon to trim board
Lemon, primrose and tangerine petal dust (blossom tint)

EQUIPMENT

36cm (14 in) oval cake board
Flat paintbrush
Flat or tilted cake stand
Posy pick

FLOWERS

1 stem of fragrant evening primrose (see page 142)
1 stem of hypericum berries (see page 78)
5 stems of large dark ivy (see page 114)
5 photinia leaves (see page 119)
1 sprig of rosemary (see page 65)

PREPARATION

1 Brush the cake with apricot glaze and cover with almond paste. Moisten the surface of the almond paste with alcohol and cover with white sugarpaste.

2 Cover the board with white sugarpaste and transfer the cake on top, making a neat join between the cake base and board. Allow to dry.

3 Mix together some lemon and primrose petal dust. Using a flat brush, dust the sides of the cake with colour starting at the base and fading the colour out at about half the depth of the cake. Add some colour to the top of the cake where the spray is to be positioned. Intensify the colour on the sides and the top by adding some tangerine petal dust.

4 Attach a band of willow green ribbon and yellow ribbon to the sides of the cake. Using the yellow and tangerine petal dust, colour half of the yellow ribbon simply by dusting on top. Glue the green velvet ribbon to the board edge, using a non-toxic glue stick.

ASSEMBLY

5 Tape together the flowers, berries and foliage for the evening primrose spray into an informal tied bunch. If you are displaying the cake flat, then simply rest the spray on top of the cake.

6 If you are using a tilted cake stand as I have used here, then you will need to attach the spray to the cake. Therefore insert a small posy pick into the cake and fill with a sausage of sugarpaste. Position the spray on to the top of the cake and over the posy pick. Bend a piece of wire to form a staple; place over the handle of the spray and insert the two ends of the staple into the sugarpaste in the posy pick. Place the cake on the tilting cake stand.

FRAGRANT EVENING PRIMROSE

Evening primroses (*Oenothera stricta*) were introduced to Great Britain and now they have naturalized themselves. There are almost 100 species, including some white and pink forms, with varying sizes of flower. Most of the species have a fragrant perfume but this form, as it name implies, is very fragrant. Flowering from June to September, evening primroses open in the late afternoon to early evening and remain open, even during dull weather. A fading flower turns a rich orange/red colour.

MATERIALS

20, 26, 28 and 30-gauge wires
Small seed-head stamens or small hammer-head stamens (optional)
Lemon, vine green, primrose, red, apricot, tangerine, dark green, moss green and aubergine petal dust (blossom tint)
Pale melon, pale green and mid-holly/ivy flower paste
½ glaze (see page 151)

EQUIPMENT

White and nile green floristry tape
Heart cutter (TT333)
Ceramic silk veining tool
Fuchsia sepal cutter (TT309)
Leaf template (see page 156)

PISTIL AND STAMENS

1 To make the pistil, tape over the end of a 30-gauge wire with ½-width white floristry tape, leaving a flap at the end. Using a fine pair of scissors, cut the flap into four. Twist each section between your finger and thumb to make fine strands. Curl the tips back slightly.

2 The stamens can either be made by cutting the ends off eight seed-head stamens and attaching a tiny strand of paste to form a 'T' bar, or use eight small hammer-heads. Tape the eight stamens around the pistil so they are a bit shorter. Dust the tips of the stamens with lemon. Tinge the tip of the pistil with vine green.

PETALS

3 Thinly roll out melon paste leaving the centre slightly thicker. Cut out a petal using the heart cutter. Insert a moistened 28-gauge white wire into the ridge to at least half the length.

4 Vein the petal using a silk veining tool. Frill the upper edge of the petal using the same tool, then soften the edge by re-frilling with a cocktail stick.

5 Pinch the upper surface to form a ridge. Repeat to make four petals. Dry with a gentle curve.

COLOURING AND ASSEMBLY

6 Before the petals have completely dried, dust them with primrose and a little lemon petal dust on the back and the front. Dust a patch of red at the very base of each petal. To make a fading flower, dust with apricot, tangerine and red.

7 Tape the petals around the stamens and pistil using ½-width floristry tape. Re-shape the petals to form a more relaxed natural finish. For a fading flower, scrunch the petals around the stamens.

CALYX

8 The calyx is very slender, so you will need to squash each of the sepals on the fuchsia sepal cutter with pliers. Form a teardrop-shaped piece of pale green paste. Pinch out the base to form a pedestal and thin out the base against the board using a celstick. Cut out the calyx shape using the re-designed fuchsia cutter. If the pedestal is too broad to fit the cutter over, place the paste on top of the cutter and rub your finger or thumb over the paste against the cutter to cut out the shape.

9 Elongate the sepals, rolling them on the board with a celstick. Hollow out and draw down a central vein on each sepal using the dresden tool. Moisten the back of the flower at the base and thread the calyx on to the back. Thin down the paste on the back of the calyx and remove excess. The sepals should lie straight down away from the petals. Dust the calyx with primrose and moss green mixed. Dust the edge with red.

BUDS

10 Roll a ball of paste into a cone shape and insert a hooked, moistened 26-gauge wire into the base. Work the paste down the wire, then thin out half of its length by rolling firmly between your fingers and thumb. Cut off excess paste. Flatten the sides of the upper half of the bud. Divide the surface of the bud into four using a scalpel. Cut the tip of the bud into four and pinch each of the sections to form four points at the tip. Pinch a ridge in between each of the indents. Dust with moss and primrose and then catch each of the pinched ridges with some red. Make buds of various sizes.

LEAVES

11 Roll out a strip of mid-green paste on to a grooved board and cut out the leaf shape. Insert a moistened 28-gauge wire into at least half the length of the leaf. Place on a pad and draw three veins on the leaf, using the fine end of the dresden tool. Soften the edges and allow to firm.

12 Dust with dark green and a touch of moss green petal dust. Dust the tip with a little red. Dip into a ½ glaze. This leaf has pale veins – etch off the glaze and colour on the leaf to reveal them if liked.

ASSEMBLY

13 Start the stem by taping a small leaf at the end of a 20-gauge wire with ½-width tape. Add a few more leaves around the stem at intervals. Introduce a small bud and where its stem joins the main stem, tape a leaf tight to the main stem. Continue to add buds and leaves, then introduce the flowers again adding a leaf at the axil. Finish with a fading flower. Dust the main stem with a little aubergine and red.

MIDSUMMER NIGHT'S DREAM

A beautiful wedding cake featuring the popular floral combination of roses, honeysuckle, ivy and hypericum berries – typical of a midsummer wedding. The sprays have been complemented with a delicate piped antique lace side design.

MATERIALS

18cm (6 in) and 25cm (10 in) oval cakes
Apricot glaze
1.75kg (3½ lb) almond paste (marzipan)
Clear alcohol (kirsch or vodka)
2.5kg (5lb) Champagne sugarpaste
Ivory coloured royal icing
Broad peach ribbon to trim boards

EQUIPMENT

20cm (8in) and 38cm (15in) oval cake boards
Nos. 0 and 2 piping tubes (tips)
Lace templates (see page 157)
A4 plastic file pocket
Firm foam
Nile green floristry tape
Pliers
Wire cutters
2 posy picks
Shallow perspex separator

FLOWERS

Small spray
1 large rose, 1 half rose, 1 rosebud and 1 set of rose leaves (see page 136-9)
3 sets of honeysuckle buds with foliage (see page 62)
3 small sets of hypericum berries with foliage (see page 78)
5 stems of ivy (see page 114)
1 sprig of rosemary (see page 65)

Large spray
5 stems of ivy
1 large rose, 1 half rose, 3 rosebuds and 2 sets of rose leaves
3 sets of honeysuckle buds with foliage
3 sets of hypericum berries with foliage
2 sprigs of rosemary

PREPARATION

1 Brush the cakes with apricot glaze and cover with almond paste. Allow to dry. Moisten the almond paste with clear alcohol and cover with champagne sugarpaste.

2 Cover the cake boards with champagne sugarpaste. Place the cakes on top, making sure they are central and that there is a neat join between the cake bases and boards. Allow to dry.

3 Using ivory coloured royal icing and a piping bag fitted with a no. 2 piping tube, pipe a snailtrail around the base of the cakes.

LACE

4 Trace the three sizes of lace design from page 157 on to a piece of tracing paper. Cut a piece of thick card to a size that will slide into an A4 plastic file pocket. Insert the card along with the tracing paper into the pocket so that the design shows through the plastic.

5 Pipe over the lace design using ivory coloured royal icing and a piping bag fitted with a no. 0 piping tube. It helps to shake a little as you pipe to create the antique quality to the lace. Pipe one large piece, 4 medium pieces and 4 small pieces for each scallop.

6 Scribe a fine line on to the cake, either freehand or using a template, to help position the lace. Using a no. 1 or 0 tube and ivory royal icing, attach the lace pieces to the cake, piping two dots. Support the lace until it has dried, using small cubes of firm foam. When dry, carefully remove the foam. Pipe a single dot in between the lace pieces.

SPRAYS

7 To form the basic outline of the large spray, bend the ends of several pieces of ivy at an angle of 90 degrees.

8 Tape the large rose into the centre of the spray to form the focal point. Tape in the three sets of honeysuckle buds, curving where required. Add and tape in the rosebuds and half rose, curving them to follow the basic shape.

9 Fill in the gaps with the hypericum berries, rose leaves, rosemary and extra pieces of ivy. Cut away any excess wires and tape over to neaten the handle of the spray. Repeat to make a slightly smaller spray for the top tier.

ASSEMBLY

10 Insert the posy picks into the cakes, then position the sprays, inserting the handles into the picks.

11 Place the divider on to the base tier and place the small cake on top. Adjust the flowers and leaves to create a balanced arrangement.

Floral Romance

This beautiful wedding cake has the exquisite combination of gerberas and roses with delicate embroidery, lace and extension work. It was designed and decorated by Norma Laver, and was displayed on the Table of Honour at the International British Sugarcraft Guild Exhibition 1997.

Materials

20cm (8 in) and 30cm (12 in) scalloped oval cakes
Apricot glaze
2kg (4lb) almond paste (marzipan)
Clear alcohol (kirsch or vodka)
3kg (6lb) white sugarpaste
White royal icing (see page 152)
Green velvet ribbon to trim boards

Equipment

25cm (10 in) and 40cm (16 in) scalloped oval cake boards
Nos. 0 and 1 piping tubes (tips)
Embroidery and lace design template (see page 158)
A4 plastic file pocket
Fine pins
2 posy picks
Perspex plinth cake stand

Flowers

8 stems of ivy (see page 114)
5 gerberas (see page 30)
12 roses (see page 136)
Assorted foliage
Several small filler flowers and buds, such as jasmine (see page 38)

Preparation

1 Brush the cakes with apricot glaze and cover with almond paste. Allow to dry for one week. Moisten the surface of the almond paste with clear alcohol and cover with white sugarpaste. Cover the cake boards with white sugarpaste and place the cakes on top. Allow to dry for a few days. Pipe a snail trail around the base of both of the cakes using white royal icing and a piping bag fitted with a no. 1 piping tube.

Side Decoration

2 Trace the lace design on page 158 and a freestyle daisy shape on to a piece of tracing paper. Cut a piece of card to fit into an A4 plastic file pocket. Insert the card with the tracing paper into the pocket so that the design shows through.

3 Pipe over the designs using white royal icing and a no. 0 piping tube. Allow to dry.

4 Make a greaseproof (parchment) paper pattern for the embroidery design and the extension work. Scribe the design on to the sides of the cakes. Using a no. 0 tube and white royal icing, pipe the embroidery design on to the cakes. Allow to dry completely.

5 Insert sterile pins into the icing evenly spaced around the cake.

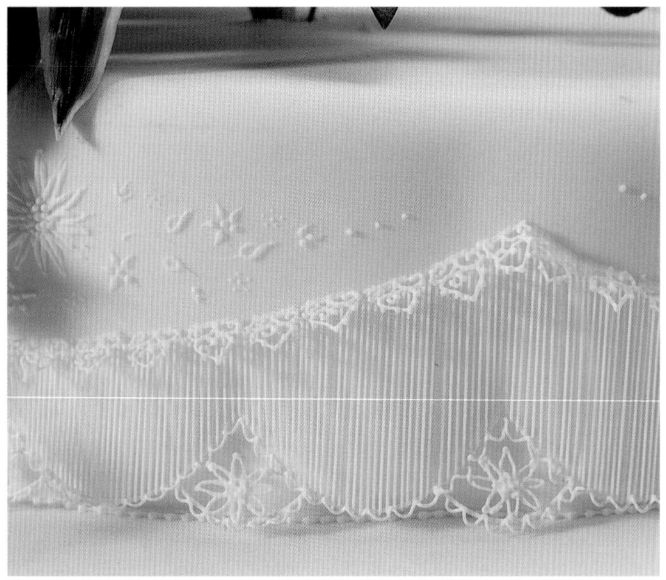

Brush a tiny amount of melted fat on to the pins. Using a no. 0 tube and fresh royal icing, pipe dropped lines from pin to pin, making the lines even in length – this forms the bridge. Allow to dry.

6 Next, pipe the threads of extension work from the cake on to the dropped line bridge. As you work around the cake and the icing dries, you can remove each of the pins in turn. Allow to dry.

7 Pipe another dropped line in between each of the scallops. Allow to dry. Remove a piece of lace from the plastic file and attach into the small scallop with a few dots of royal icing. Repeat to complete both of the cakes.

8 Pipe tiny scallops over the dropped scalloped bridge. Dry, then attach the daisy lace pieces.

9 Attach the lace on to the cake just above the extension work. Attach the green velvet ribbon to the board edges using a non-toxic glue stick, taking care not to damage the extension work and lace.

ASSEMBLY

10 You will need to make two sprays for this cake. Bend the end of two stems of ivy to a 90 degree angle, taping them together to form a semi-crescent shape and a handle at the centre of the spray. Tape in some extra ivy stems in the same way to form the basic outline of the spray.

11 Tape in the gerberas using one of the flowers as a focal point. Add the roses to fill in the gaps in the spray. Add depth and fill in the backs of the sprays with assorted plain and variegated foliage and a few jasmine flowers and buds.

12 Insert a posy pick into each cake. Position the handle of each spray in them.

13 Place the small cake on top of the perspex plinth stand and position the larger cake in front of the stand.

EQUIPMENT AND TECHNIQUES

This basic list of equipment is required to make the sugar flowers and foliage used in the book. Any special pieces of equipment needed to make specific cakes or flowers is listed with each set of instructions. Most of the equipment is available from specialist cake decorating suppliers.

EQUIPMENT

Board and Rolling Pin

A non-stick board and rolling pin are essential for rolling out flower paste thinly. I prefer to work on a dark green non-stick board, as a white board strains your eyes if you are working for long periods of time. If you are making a lot of flowers and foliage, then you might prefer to use a grooved board or rolling pin to create thick central ridges on petals and leaves to allow the wires to be inserted, rather than using the other method as described in Techniques. These are available commercially, but you can also make grooves yourself in the back of a non-stick board. To do this, heat a metal skewer until it turns red hot, then brand the back of the board several times until you have achieved a groove of the required depth and width. I find that one long groove across the board is most useful, plus a smaller finer groove at one side of the board. Scrape off any excess plastic, and then smooth the board with some fine glass paper.

Foam Pads

These are used to hold paste while you soften or vein a petal or leaf. There are several pads that are commercially available. If you are planning to buy a pad for the first time, it must be firm and have a fine texture – there are several brands that are too rough and can easily tear the edges of the paste.

Dresden/Veining Tool

My personal favourite is the black dresden/veining tool made by Jem. The fine end of the tool is used for drawing veins down the centre of petals, sepals and leaves. The broad end is used to draw veins and to hollow out the edges and centres of petals and leaves. The broad end is also used to create an effect known as 'double frilling'. This gives a 'ridged look' and, if worked to a certain degree, is ideal for creating jagged or ragged edges to leaves and petals.

Celsticks

These are available in four sizes: small, medium, large and extra large. One end of each tool is pointed; the other is rounded. The pointed end is used to open up the centres of flowers and can also be used for veining. The rounded end is used like the bone-end tool, but with the advantage of a range of different sized tools for the various sizes of flowers and leaves. The central part of each of the celsticks can also be used as a rolling pin for flowers formed from a pedestal shape. They are also regularly used for rolling thick ridges on paste needed for wired petals and leaves.

Pliers and Wire Cutters

Small fine-nosed pliers are essential, but a good pair will cost you between £25–£30! They are a delight to use and when you buy a pair you often wonder how you managed without them! They can be purchased from specialist electrical supply shops. Wire cutters are also very useful; either electrical cutters or a pair of heavy duty florist's scissors.

Floristry Tape

Paper floristry tape is available in many colours but I use mainly nile green, white, beige and twig. The tape has a glue in it that is released when the paper is stretched, so it is important to stretch the tape firmly as you tape over a wire.

Florists' Staysoft

This is basically plasticine, but it is sold by florists' suppliers and some cake-decorating shops in long blocks. It is easier to arrange flowers into this medium, as they can be removed and re-arranged if a mistake is made (as the name implies - it stays soft). Blocks of green can also be obtained from good art shops. If you are planning to use this medium, it must be arranged on to a container or disc so that it does not come into immediate contact with the cake.

Tape Shredder

This is used to cut lengths of floristry tape into various widths. If you remove one of the blades, you will have a shredder that will cut one half and two quarter width lengths at the same time. The blades are actually razor blades and will need to be replaced from time to time.

Wires

The quality of the wires available varies; it is best to buy A-grade wire, which can be identified by a red spot on the packet. Although it is more expensive I advise you to use only this wire. I personally now only buy white wire in gauges from 33-gauge (fine) to 24-gauge (thicker), preferring to tape over the wire with nile green tape during the assembly of the flower. There are also stronger wires available from 22-gauge to 14-gauge wire (the higher the number the finer the wire). These can be covered or uncovered, it does not matter which you use. You can also buy very fine silk-covered 36-gauge wire on a reel, which is ideal for very small flowers.

Great Impressions (GI) Veiners

These are double-sided rubber veiners moulded from real flowers and foliage. They add a great deal of realism to flower work. Once you have cut out the leaf or petal and inserted a wire (see right), place the shape into the veiner (the ridge on the paste should fit into the back piece of the veiner). Press the two sides together firmly and then remove the leaf, now veined on both sides to natural perfection. You will need to assess the thickness of paste required for some of the more heavily veined petals and leaves – if you make the paste too fine the veiner might cut the paste!

Ceramic Silk Veining Tool (HP)

This tool has veins on the surface; when rolled over the paste it gives a delicate texture. It can also frill the edges of petals, veining them at the same time.

Cutters

There are many different types of cutters available. Cutters speed up the flower-making process and help to add consistency and accuracy easily to your work. I use mainly metal cutters as there are

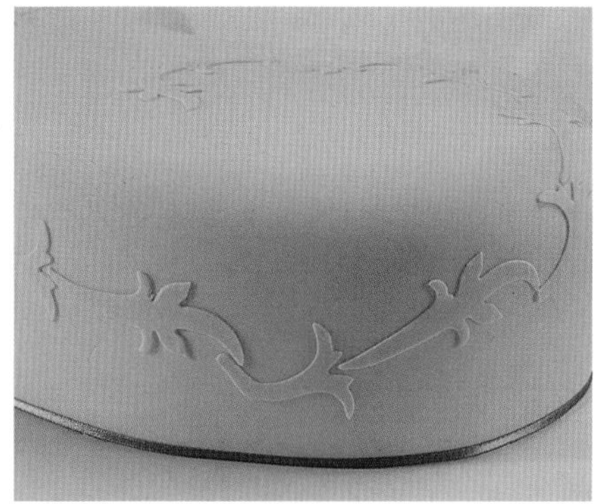

more shapes available, plus if I need to alter the shape of a cutter I can adjust the shape using pliers. I also have a large range of plastic cutters. For many forms of foliage I prefer to use these as they can often be more intricate in shape. The majority of the cutters used in this book are readily available from most good cake decorating shops. Some cutters however can be difficult to buy and you will need to order these. See page 160 for suppliers.

Thread

Fine white lace-making cotton thread (Brock 120) is best used for stamens, although some thicker cotton threads can also be useful.

Stamens

There is a vast range of stamens available to the flower maker. I use mainly white stamens, preferring to colour them to the required colour as I need them. I always keep a supply of small white seed-head stamens and some finer white stamens.

Paintbrushes

Good brushes are essential, although they don't necessarily have to be very expensive. They are one of the most important items in a flower-maker's kit. Remember that the final control and accuracy with colouring can make or break your work. Flat brushes are the most useful for dusting flowers and foliage (round brushes are not firm enough to colour accurately with petal dust/blossom tint). Recently I have been using brushes by Robert Simmons called Craft Painters nos. 6 and 8. You will need a good selection of finer brushes for painting fine details on flowers and foliage.

Low Heat Glue Gun

This is an item of equipment that can be very useful for gluing florists' staysoft or oasis to boards and stands. The glue sticks are fed into the gun and, when the glue is hot, it can be eased through the gun on to the object you need gluing. Although it operates at a lower temperature, you still need to be careful not to burn your fingers. This can also be used for gluing stamens on to wires for flowers with very neat shallow or fine backs. Do not use for competition work.

Hi-tack Glue

This is a non-toxic glue that can also be used to glue stamens on to wire and glue florists' staysoft on to boards etc. It should not come into immediate contact with the surface of the cakes but is quite safe to use on flowers with wires in them. Do not use for competition work.

TECHNIQUES

Wiring Leaves and Petals

Roll out some flower paste to the required thickness leaving a thick ridge down the centre – this can either be achieved by rolling a piece of well kneaded paste with a large celstick, leaving the centre thicker or by rolling out the paste on a grooved board. I prefer to use the first method if I have time, as the finished result is often neater and stronger. Cut out the petal or leaf shape using a cutter or template. You will need to position the cutter so that the ridge of paste runs from the tip to the base of the leaf or petal. Press the cutter down firmly, then release the paste from the cutter. (I often find that I end up with cleaner cut edges if I scrub the cutter and paste against the board.) Moisten the end of a wire and insert it into the thick ridge, holding the paste firmly between your finger and thumb to prevent the end of the wire coming through. Insert the wire into at least half the length of the ridge to give support.

Colouring

I use a small selection of paste food colourings to colour flower paste, preferring to alter and colour the flowers and foliage with petal dusts (blossom tints) after shaping. Petal dusts can also be mixed into flower paste to colour it, but if used in large proportions they can alter the consistency too much. I usually colour the paste a paler shade of the colour that I want the finished flower to be, then dust on top to achieve more depth and realistic effects. It is important to have a good selection of petal dust colours and to experiment with different colour combinations to obtain the effect you want. I rarely use only one colour on a flower or leaf. The colours can either be mixed together or simply brushed on to the paste in layers. The instructions for each of the flowers in this book include a list of colours used. I am very fond of green and so most of my cakes have a lot of foliage on them. In the instructions I often mention a dark green mixture which adds a lot of depth to foliage. To achieve the depth of green required, mix together equal proportions of moss green and jade, and then darken with nutkin brown and a little black. I usually mix up a large pot of colour in advance, rather than mixing up small amounts of dust at a time as this wastes both time and dust!

If you want to make a colour a paler shade, it will need to mixed with white petal dust. Sometimes a little cornflour

(cornstarch) is added, but this is usually to clean the colour out of a brush to give a very, very subtle tinge of colour to the tips of petals (usually it involves green and primrose petal dust). I use only a few liquid colours, the main one being cyclamen, to paint detail spots and lines on to petals.

Glazing

There are several ways to add a glaze to flowers and leaves; I use only two. The steaming method is used not to give a high gloss, more to create a 'waxy' finish or, more often, to remove the dry dusted appearance left by petal dust. It is also used when trying to create a velvety finish or darken the depth of colour of a flower or a leaf, since the surface of the paste is still slightly damp after steaming. Hold each flower or leaf in the steam from a boiling kettle for a few seconds, or until the surface turns shiny. Take great care as too much steam can soften and dissolve the sugar. For a more permanent and shiny glaze, use confectioners' varnish. Used neat (full glaze), this

gives a high gloss, which is ideal for berries and glossy leaves. However, for most foliage this looks too artificial, so it is better to dilute the varnish with iso-propyl alcohol (available from chemists). Confectioners' varnish is actually made from a base of iso-propyl alcohol and shellac. Mix the varnish and alcohol in a lidded container and shake to mix – not too much as this will form tiny air bubbles. The glaze may be used straight away. Simply dip the leaf, petal or a group of pieces into the glaze, shake off the excess and dry on absorbent kitchen paper. The glaze may be applied with a paintbrush, but I find the brush strokes tend to remove the colour in streaks. The following glazes are those most often used.

¼ glaze

Three-quarters alcohol to a quarter part varnish. This is used for leaves that don't have much shine; the glaze just takes away the flat, dusty look of a leaf or petal.

½ glaze

Equal proportions of alcohol and varnish. This gives a natural shine that is ideal for many foliages, including ivy and rose leaves.

¾ glaze

Quarter part alcohol to three-quarters varnish. This gives a semi-gloss without the 'plastic' appearance of a full glaze.

Using a 'Cage'

A wire 'cage' is used to mark the impression of unopened petals on a bud. The 'cage' is made from wire, the gauge depending on the size of the bud. If you are making the bud of a five-petalled flower, you will need five pieces of wire for the 'cage'. Tape the pieces of wire together at one end with ½-width floristry tape and open up the cage, trying not to cross the wires at the base. Insert the modelled bud, tip or base first, depending on the effect required. Close the wires on to its surface, keeping them as evenly spaced as possible. For some buds, a more realistic effect is achieved if the paste between the wires is pinched out and thinned with your finger and thumb to form a ridge that gives the appearance of larger petals. After removing from the 'cage', twist to give a spiral effect.

Flower Paste

The type of flower paste you use is a matter of personal preference. I prefer a paste that stretches well and does not dry out on the surface too fast, allowing me to wire petals together whilst they are still damp (a factor that most pastes fall down on). I now always buy ready-made flower paste (by mail order) because it is more consistent than home-made paste, and it saves me a lot of time and trouble. Make your own from the following recipe if you wish.

25ml (5 teaspoons) cold water
10ml (2 teaspoons) powdered gelatine
500g (1lb/3 cups) icing (confectioners') sugar, sifted
15ml (3 teaspoons) gum tragacanth
10ml (2 teaspoons) liquid glucose
15ml (3 teaspoons) white vegetable fat (shortening)
1 medium egg white (preferably free-range)

1 Mix the water and gelatine together in a small heatproof bowl and leave to stand for 30 minutes. Sift the icing sugar and gum tragacanth into the bowl of a heavy-duty mixer and fit the bowl to the machine.

2 Place the bowl with the gelatine mixture over a saucepan of hot water and stir until the gelatine has dissolved. Warm a teaspoon in hot water, then measure out the liquid glucose (the heat should help to ease the glucose off the spoon). Add the glucose and white fat to the gelatine mixture, and continue to heat until all of the ingredients have melted and are thoroughly mixed together.

3 Add the dissolved gelatine mixture to the icing sugar, along with the egg white. Fit the beater to the machine and

turn it on at its lowest speed. Beat until mixed, then increase the speed to maximum until the paste is white and stringy.

4 Remove the paste from the bowl and rub a thin layer of white fat over it to prevent the outer part drying out. Place in a plastic bag and store in an airtight container. Allow the paste to rest and mature for at least 12 hours before using it.

Working with Flower Paste

You will need a pot of fresh egg white, a pot of cornflour (cornstarch) and white vegetable fat. There has been a trend over recent years to use gum arabic solution, gum glues, water and alcohol as replacements for egg white (because of the salmonella scares). I have continued to use fresh egg white as it is far superior to any of the alternatives.

1 The paste should be kneaded well before it is modelled into a flower or rolled out on a board, otherwise it has a tendency to dry out and crack around the edges. If the paste is dry or tough, then soften it using fresh egg white (not gum arabic etc) – do not add white fat in large quantities as this will make the paste short, difficult to work with and it will take longer to dry.

2 If the paste is sticky then a small amount of white fat may be used on the fingers while you knead it – but do not add too much! For many people the temptation when the paste is sticky is to add cornflour (cornstarch); while cornflour can be used on the surface of the paste quite happily, if it is added to flower paste it seems to aggravate the stickiness.

3 Always grease the board with white fat, then remove almost completely with absorbent kitchen paper. This will form a very thin layer of fat on the board and stop the paste gripping to the board. If you use too much fat it will show up on the finished petal or leaf when you petal dust as a darker patch.

4 Although the commercial paste that I use does not dry out very quickly, it is advisable if you are cutting out a large number of petals to cover them with a celflap or a plastic bag to stop the surface crusting over.

Royal Icing with dried albumen

This royal icing recipe is suitable for coating, piping a snail trail, and shells, runouts, brush embroidery etc. It makes about 2kg (4lb) of icing.

45g (3 tablespoons) pure dried albumen powder
315ml (10floz/1¼ cups) water
1.75kg (3½lb/10½ cups) icing (confectioners') sugar, sifted

1 Wash the mixer bowl, a small bowl and the beater with a concentrated detergent and scald to remove any grease and leftover detergent.

2 Reconstitute the dried albumen with the water in a small bowl or other container. It will become very lumpy, but do not worry about it, just stir it and leave it to dissolve for about 20 minutes. Strain the mixture into the mixer bowl.

3 Add the sifted icing sugar gradually and mix it into the albumen. Fix the bowl and beater to the electric mixer and beat on the slowest speed for 4 minutes (soft peak) or 5 minutes (full peak).

Royal Icing (with fresh egg white)

This recipe is intended for fine lace work and long extension work, although I have been known to use it for embroidery, snail trail, shells and brush embroidery, omitting the tartaric and acetic acids. These are added to the egg white to alter the PH balance of the egg whites.

1 medium egg white (preferably free-range and at room temperature)
Pinch of tartaric acid (for fine lace work)
or 2 drops of acetic acid (for long dropped lines of extension work)
225g (8oz/1¾ cups) icing (confectioners') sugar, sifted

1 Wash and scald the bowl and beater as described before. Place the egg white into the bowl with the pinch of tartaric acid. Add the majority of the icing sugar and mix the two together.

2 Fix the bowl and beater to the machine and beat on the slowest speed until it has reached full peak, this takes about 8 minutes. You might need to mix in some more sugar if the mixture is too soft.

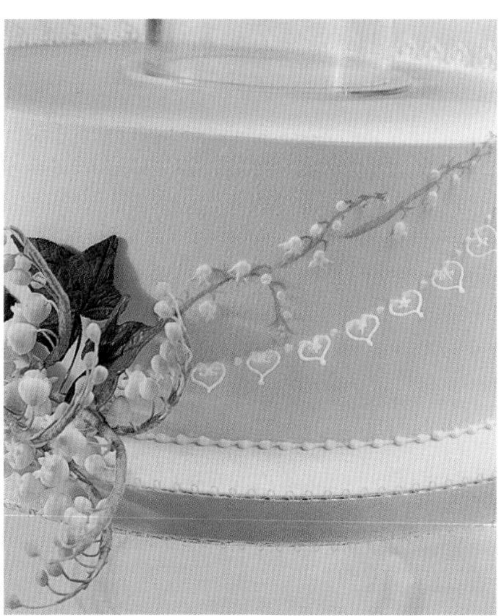

Coating with Sugarpaste

1 Knead the sugarpaste to make it smooth: try not to knead too many air bubbles into it. Lightly dust the work surface with icing (confectioners') sugar. Roll out the sugarpaste to an even thickness, about 1cm (½ in). Moisten the surface of the almond paste with clear alcohol (vodka, kirsch, cointreau etc). Form an even coating of alcohol – if you have dry areas then these are prone to form air bubbles with the sugarpaste.

2 Lift the sugarpaste over the cake and ease into position, smoothing out the top to remove air bubbles before working on the sides. Trim the sugarpaste from around the base of the cake. Polish the top and the sides of the cake using sugarpaste smoothers. I also use a pad of sugarpaste pressed into the palm of my hand to smooth the edges and corners of the cake. If you catch the paste and make an indent, try smoothing over with the pad of paste as it often disguises the fault quickly.

Covering a Cake Board with Sugarpaste

Moisten the cake board with a small amount of boiled water or clear alcohol. Roll out sufficient sugarpaste to cover the board. Trim the edge. Soften the cut edge using the sugarpaste smoother.

If you are concerned about the cake and the sugarpaste on the board becoming sticky in between being decorated and the cake-cutting ceremony, you have several options. Firstly, you can cut out the sugarpaste from the board the same shape and size of the cake, then position the cake on top. Alternatively, place the cake on a thin board of the same size and shape before it is almond-pasted and sugarpasted, then position it on to the larger sugarpasted board.

The Parts of a Flower

Throughout this book, reference is made to the various parts of a flower. The illustration and following notes will help you identify them.

Pistil

This is the female part of a flower and is made up of a stigma, style and ovary. The pistil varies in its formation between the various different flowers. In some flowers, such as a lily, the pistil can be large.

Stamens

The stamens provide the male part of a flower and are made up of a filament and a pollen-covered anther.

Petals

These are usually the most attractive, coloured parts of a flower, their main purpose being to attract insects to the flower.

Tepals

These look like petals and appear in flowers that have no calyx, such as anemone, hellebore or lily.

Calyx and Sepals

The calyx is made up of several individual sepals. It is the outer layer of a bud that protects the flower while it is forming inside.

Bract

This is located where the flower stem joins the main stem. It is a small, modified leaf (intermediate between the sepals and the leaves).

Spadix

This is a fleshy axis that carries both male and female flowers, such as the centre of an arum lily or anthurium.

Spathe

This is a large petal-like bract that is usually wrapped around or positioned below the spadix of the arum lily and anthurium.

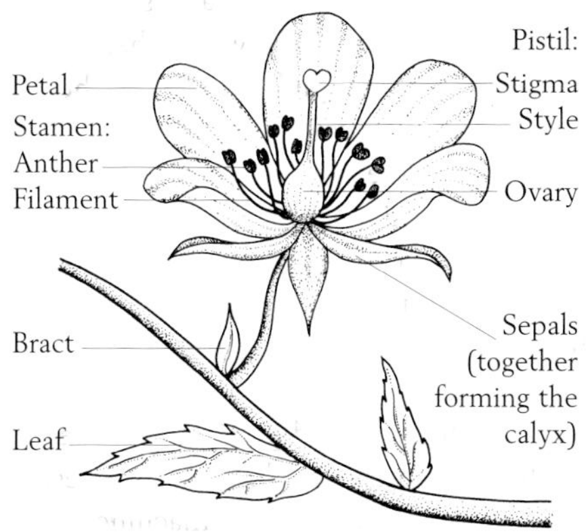

Templates

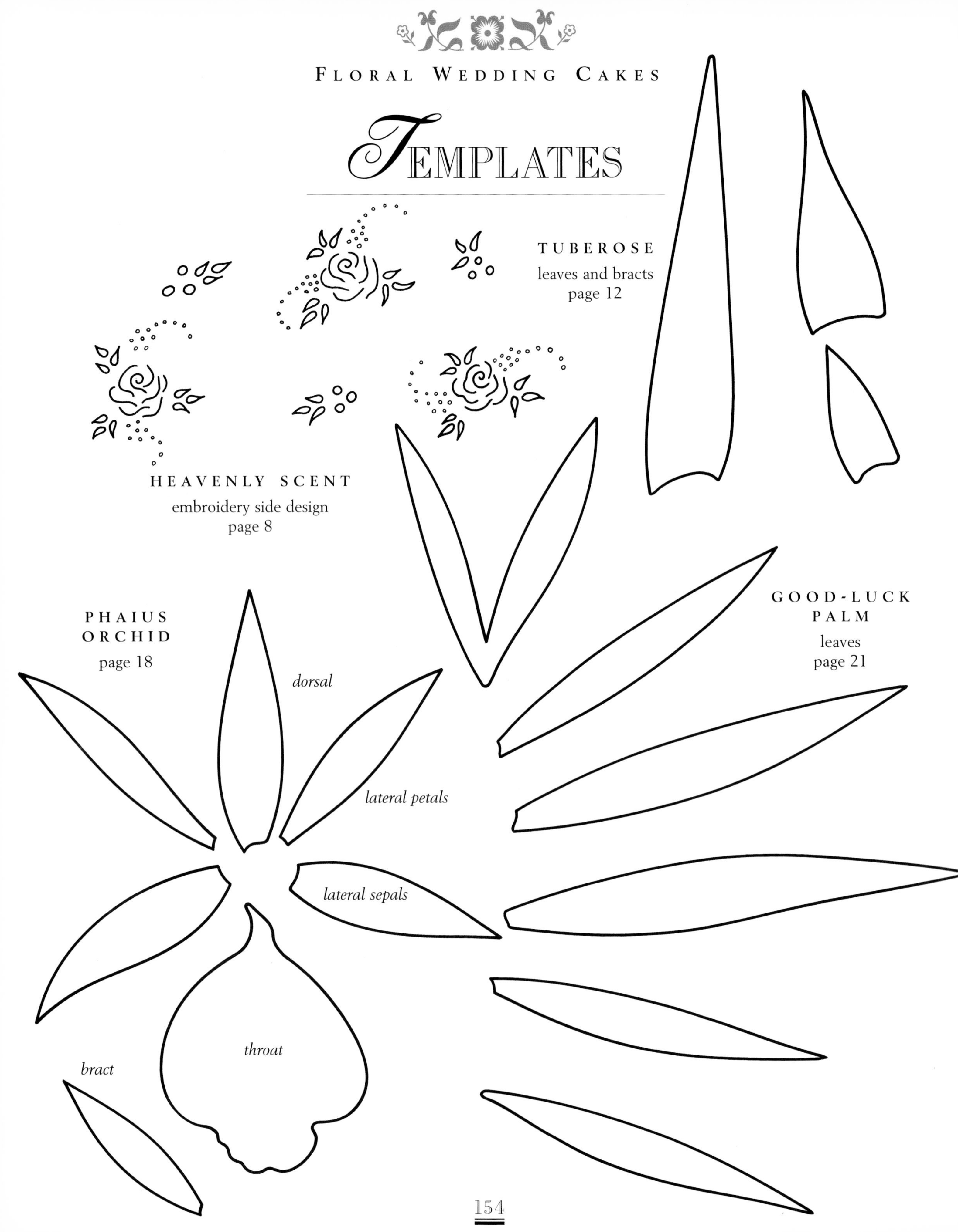
TUBEROSE
leaves and bracts
page 12
HEAVENLY SCENT
embroidery side design
page 8
GOOD-LUCK
PALM
leaves
page 21
PHAIUS
ORCHID
page 18
dorsal
lateral petals
lateral sepals
throat
bract

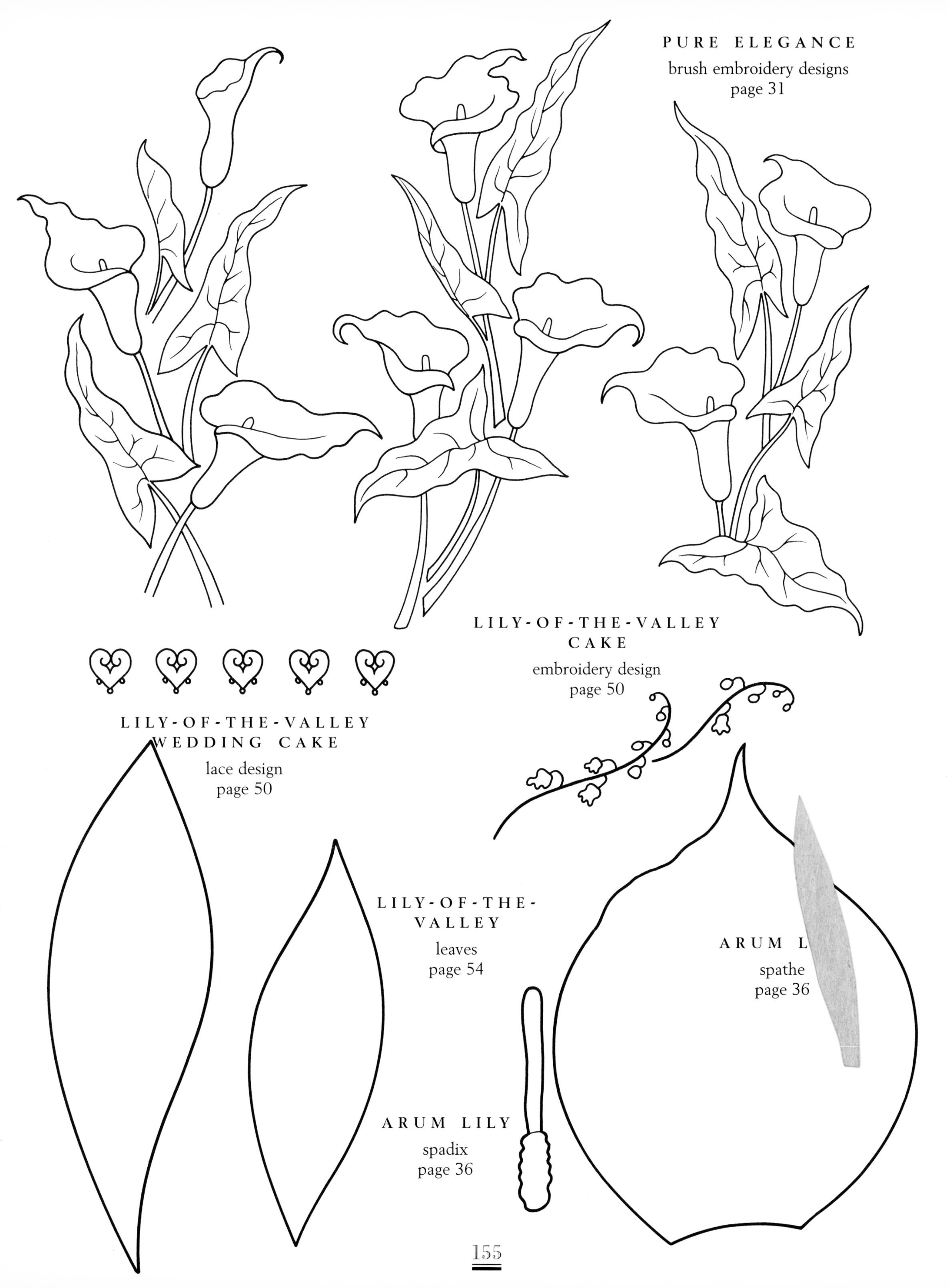
PURE ELEGANCE
brush embroidery designs
page 31
LILY-OF-THE-VALLEY CAKE
embroidery design
page 50
LILY-OF-THE-VALLEY WEDDING CAKE
lace design
page 50
LILY-OF-THE-VALLEY
leaves
page 54
ARUM L
spathe
page 36
ARUM LILY
spadix
page 36

SWEET PEA

petals
page 46

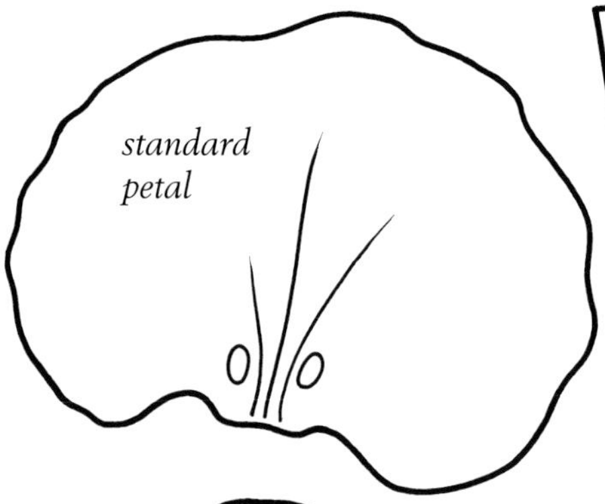

standard petal

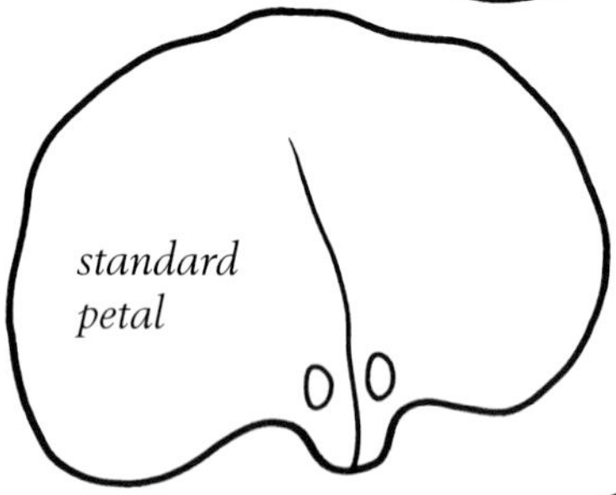

standard petal

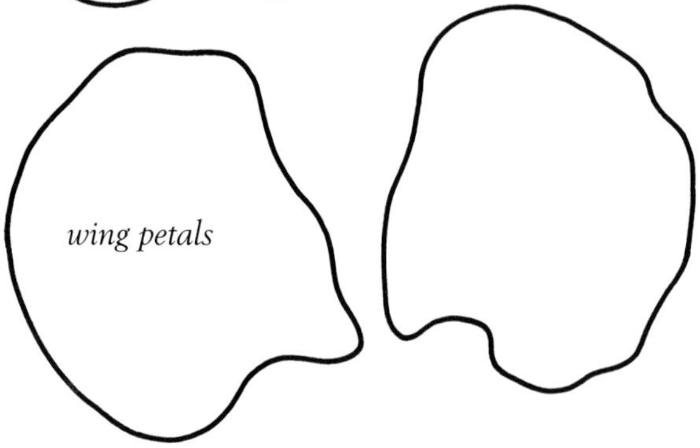

wing petals

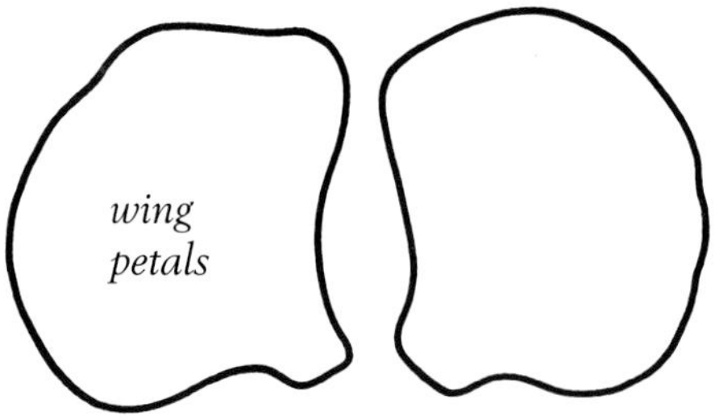

wing petals

AMARYLLIS

petals
page 80

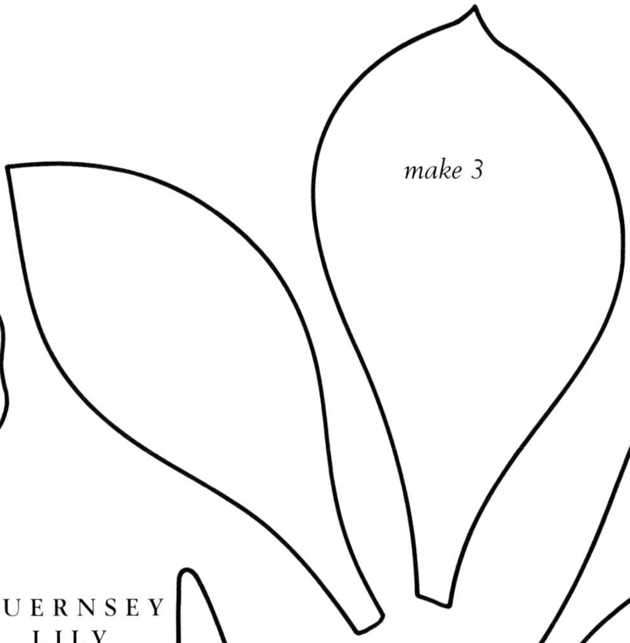

make 3

GUERNSEY LILY

petal
page 132

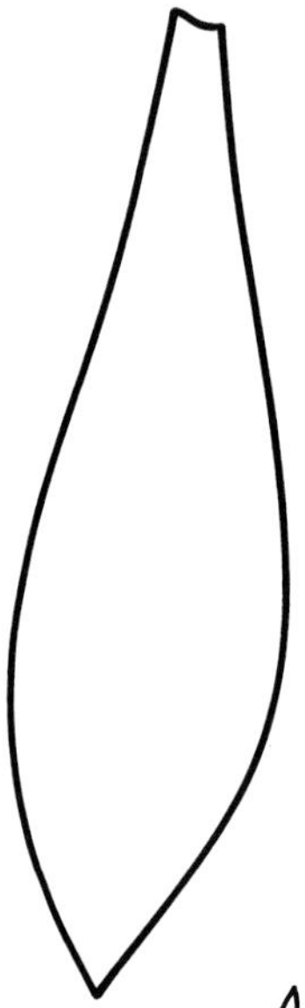

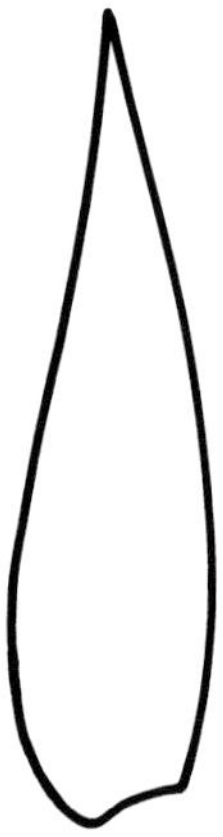

FRAGRANT EVENING PRIMROSE

leaf
page 144

FLORAL RHAPSODY

embroidery side design
page 66

RANUNCULUS

leaves
page 72

PEONY
leaves
page 124
PEONY
petals
page 124
PEONY
calyx
page 124
MIDSUMMER
NIGHT'S
DREAM
lace page 144
PEONY
WEDDING
CAKE
brush
embroidery
page 122

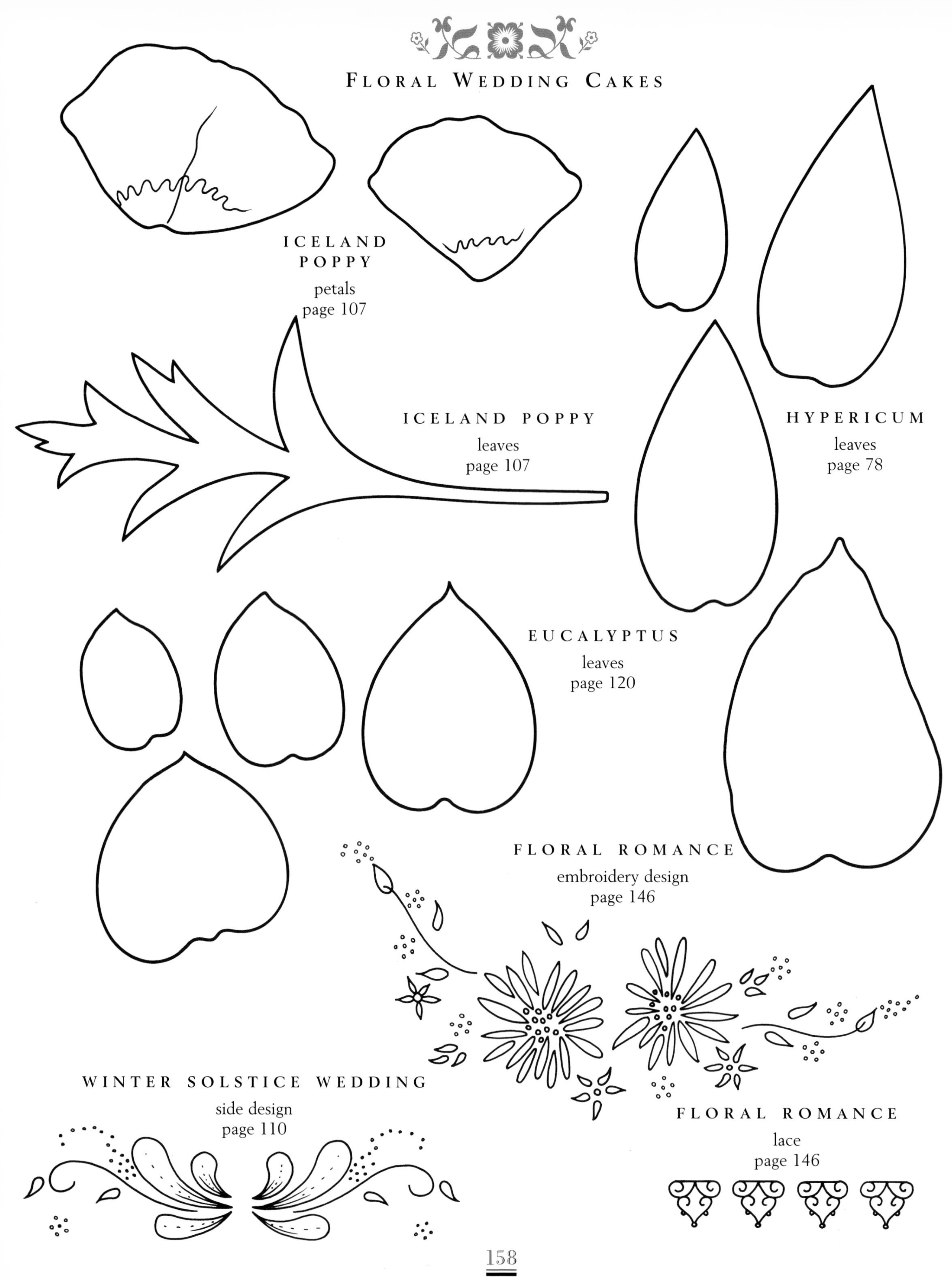
ICELAND POPPY
petals
page 107
ICELAND POPPY
leaves
page 107
HYPERICUM
leaves
page 78
EUCALYPTUS
leaves
page 120
FLORAL ROMANCE
embroidery design
page 146
WINTER SOLSTICE WEDDING
side design
page 110
FLORAL ROMANCE
lace
page 146

INDEX

ACKNOWLEDGEMENTS

This book would not have been finished when it was, without the help, support, faith and tolerance of my friends listed below.

My most humble and grateful thanks go to them all. I appreciate their help and am indebted to them all.

Thank you to Alice Christie who has been a constant help throughout the writing of this book (and the previous two)!! And to Tombi Peck for her help and sense of humour during the last crucial and exhausting week of photography – it has been proven once again that we work well together under extreme last-minute pressure; to Norma Laver for the orange conversations and getting me out of a tight corner by allowing her Table of Honour cake (see page 146) to be included in this book, and also to Tony Warren for his 'you-can-do-it' phone calls, and for allowing me to use his Table of Honour cake (see page 84); to Peter Stott for his support over the years, and for flat icing (with his natural perfection) the royal iced cake.

Thank you to the following for supplying the various items used: to Renshaws Ltd for the Regalice used to cover all of the sugarpaste cakes in this book; to Margaret and David Ford of Celcakes for the perspex tube cake stands; to Beverley Dutton of Squires Kitchen for the almost never ending supply of holly/ivy petal dust and the use of the cake knife; to Paula Stock for allowing me to use her cutwork cutters on the Orchid Inspiration cake (see page 14); to June Twelves of Holly Products for the silk veining tool; to Joan Mooney of Great Impressions for the veiners; to Sally Harris of Tinkertech for the metal cutters; to John Quai Hoi for the perspex flower stand used with the cake on page 110; to Brenda Munger for sharing her tip with the Iceland poppy ovary (see page 107); to Wendy Mabbot and the gang at Cooks Corner. Thanks to Jenny, Norma and Co. at A Piece of Cake for their excellent service and friendly banter. Also thanks to Peggie Green for her very kind hospitality.

Once again my thanks to Sue Atkinson for her patience, kindness and superb photography (working miracles when required) which is equally important to this book as it was to the previous two collaborations.

Thanks also to Barbara Croxford, my editor, for her help in turning my sometimes chaotic ramblings into an organized text; and to Anita Ruddell for her design work and support for the Iceland Poppy Cake campaign.

And finally thank you once again to my long suffering parents, Allen and Avril, and my sister, Sue, for their continuing support.

The author and publishers would like to thank the following suppliers:

Anniversary House
(Cake Decorations) Ltd
Unit 5a
Roundways
Elliott Road
Bournemouth BH11 8JJ
Tel: 01202 590222

A Piece of Cake
(Mail order flowerpaste, etc)
18 Upper High Street
Thame
Oxon OX9 3EX
Tel & fax: 0184 421 3428

Cake Art Ltd
Venture Way
Crown Estate
Priorswood
Taunton
Somerset TA2 8DE
Tel: 01823 321532

Cakes, Classes and Cutters
23 Princes Road
Brunton Park
Gosforth
Newcastle-Upon-Tyne
NE3 5TT
Tel & Fax:0191 217 0538

Celcakes and Celcrafts
(Cel products, perspex stands and Asi-es products)
Springfield House
Gate Helmsley
York, Yorkshire YO4 1NF
Tel: 01759 371 447

Cooks Corner
35 Percy Street
Newcastle-Upon-Tyne
Tyne & Wear
Tel: 0191 261 5481

Country Cutters
Lower Tresaldu
Dingestow
Monmouth, Gwent NP5 4BQ
Tel: 01600 740448

Creating Cakes
The Cake Decorating Centre
63 East Street
Sittingbourne
Kent ME10 4BQ
Tel: 01795 426358

Elegant Cutwork Collection
1007 Lochmoor Blvd
Grosse Ptd Woods
NJ 48236, USA

Fleurtatious (Flower shop)
58 Acorn Road
Jesmond
Newcastle-upon-Tyne
Tel: 0191 281 3127

Great Impressions
(veiners and moulds)
14 Studley Drive
Swarland, Morpeth
Northumberland NE65 9JT
Tel & Fax:01670 787 061

Guy, Paul and Co. Ltd
Unit B4, Foundry Way
Little End Road
Eaton Socon
Cambs PE19 3SH
Tel: 01480 472545

Holly Products
(Silk veining tools etc)
Holly Cottage
Hassall Green
Cheshire CW11 4YA
Tel & Fax:01270 761 403

JF Renshaw Ltd
Crown Street
Liverpool L8 7RF
Tel: 0151 706 8200

W Robertson
The Brambles
Ryton
Tyne & Wear NE40 3AN
Tel: 0191 413 8144

Squires Kitchen
Squires House
3 Waverley Lane
Farnham
Surrey GU9 8BB
Tel: 01252 711749

Sugar Celebrations
80 Westgate Street
Gloucester GL1 2NZ
Tel: 01452 308848

The British Sugarcraft Guild
National Office
Wellington House
Messeter Place
Eltham
London SE9 5DP
Tel: 0181 859 6943
Fax: 0181 859 6117

The Flower Basket
10 High Street
Much Wenlock
Shropshire
Tel: 01952 728 101

The Old Bakery
Kingston St Mary
Taunton
Somerset TA2 8HW
Tel: 01823 451205

The Secret Garden
(Flower shop)
17 Clayton Road
Jesmond
Tyne & Wear
Tel: 0191 281 7753

The Stencil Library
Stocksfield Hall
Stocksfield
Northumberland

Tinkertech Two
(Metal cutters)
40 Langdon Road
Parkstone
Poole
Dorset BH14 9EH
Tel: 01202 738 049